# INNOVATION IN THE SCHOOLHOUSE

# Similar Works by Rowman & Littlefield's Education Division:

*From the Ground Up: Entrepreneurial School Leadership* by Jeffrey R. Cornwall

*The Entrepreneurial Educator* by Robert J. Brown and Jeffrey R. Cornwall

*Disciplining the Arts: Teaching Entrepreneurship in Context* edited by Gary D. Beckman

*Social Entrepreneurship in Education: Private Ventures for the Public Good* by Michael R. Sandler

*Working for Kids: Educational Leadership as Inquiry and Invention* by James H. Lytle

# INNOVATION IN THE SCHOOLHOUSE

## *Entrepreneurial Leadership in Education*

## Jack Leonard

ROWMAN & LITTLEFIELD EDUCATION
A DIVISION OF:
ROWMAN & LITTLEFIELD
Lanham • Boulder • New York • Toronto • Plymouth, UK

Published by Rowman & Littlefield Education
A division of Rowman & Littlefield
4501 Forbes Boulevard, Suite 200, Lanham, Maryland 20706
www.rowman.com

10 Thornbury Road, Plymouth PL6 7PP, United Kingdom

British Library Cataloguing in Publication Information Available

**Library of Congress Cataloging-in-Publication Data**

Leonard, Jack, 1948–
Innovation in the schoolhouse : entrepreneurial leadership in education / Jack Leonard.
pages cm
Includes bibliographical references and index.
ISBN 978-1-4758-0289-4 (cloth : alk. paper)—ISBN 978-1-4758-0290-0 (pbk. : alk. paper)—ISBN 978-1-4758-0291-7 (electronic)
1. Educational innovations. 2. Entrepreneurship. I. Title.
LB1027.L46 2013
371.2—dc23
2013018700

♾™ The paper used in this publication meets the minimum requirements of American National Standard for Information Sciences Permanence of Paper for Printed Library Materials, ANSI/NISO Z39.48-1992.

Printed in the United States of America

# CONTENTS

# PREFACE

This is a book about entrepreneurial leadership in K–12 education. There are many issues that have kept public education in the nation's spotlight for the past thirty years, including how our students rank on international tests, school choice, and the preparation and quality of our teachers. Despite billions of dollars and countless educational reforms, scholars both conservative and progressive have decried the tired rehash of failed educational policies.[1]

Whatever position one takes in these debates—and I tend to think these arguments miss the mark—there are more obvious and persistent problems that should trouble us. Too many students grow up in poverty and arrive unprepared for school. Equitable school funding remains elusive, even after twenty years of court cases. The full inclusion of students with disabilities and English language learners, who are growing in number, is an ongoing challenge.

We worry about the physical health of our students, shrinking schedules for the arts and physical education, bullying, and the lack of character education. Our graduation rates are too low, and too many students head off to college without being ready.

Schools have always been a bastion of stability and tradition in America, but for all the reasons above, there is a need for fresh ideas and new approaches. There is a call for innovation and for leaders who can think outside the box—for entrepreneurial leaders. This is leadership that respects meaningful traditions and does not disparage history, but has a healthy dissatisfaction with persistent problems and helps us see new ways of doing things.

## CLARIFICATIONS

There is a lot of entrepreneurial activity that swirls *around* K–12 education. Education is an enormous enterprise, second only to health care in the United States.[2] Naturally, there are businesses that address every aspect of education, including curriculum, technology, facilities, transportation, and food services from kindergarten through high school. These services are widely accepted.

In recent years, some entrepreneurs have tried to jump-start the pace of change through highly publicized initiatives, which focus on personalizing education, increasing parental choice, or improving teacher and administrator preparation and practice. Private enterprises, such as Teach for America or New Leaders for New Schools, have had significant effects on educational policy and practice. Charter management organizations such as Advantage, Green Dot, and Edison run dozens of public schools and yet promise a profit for unseen investors.

Using entrepreneurship in the same sentence with public education raises eyebrows. Many people are already upset with neoliberal policies in education, the incursion of cut-throat business practices, and all the implications of privatization, metrics, competition, and impersonal policies. Isn't entrepreneurial leadership more of this?

Usually, when scholars write about educational entrepreneurship, they have in mind the clever entrepreneurs who work on the fringes of public education.[3] In contrast, I wrote this book thinking of the people who work inside our public schools—the teachers, administrators, guidance counselors, student support staff, and all the myriad other roles—who may not self-identify as entrepreneurs. This book takes the position that entrepreneurial leadership is already prevalent inside K–12 schooling, far more common than believed, but is often overlooked, hindered, squelched, or undeveloped.

One thing about entrepreneurial thinking is that it tends to bubble up from ranks rather than trickle down from the top of the organization. This is another kind of leadership, demonstrated by imagination, independence, risk-taking, and courage to head in a new direction. In too many instances, school districts are not set up to recognize or even tolerate this kind of leadership. No wonder so many entrepreneurs find they have to break away in order to spread their wings.

For this reason, this is a book on leadership that is not particularly aimed at the people at the top of the educational hierarchy. I have watched teachers, year after year, brainstorm new and brilliant ways to reach their students. I have watched school principals find novel ways to steer meager resources into new and more productive solutions for student learning. The churning of creative energy is right there, often hampered with limited resources and frustrated with lack of recognition and appreciation, but still there.

Obviously, this is not another blame-the-teachers or a blame-the-administrators book. For all the reasons listed earlier, radical changes are needed, and we know that if we keep doing the same things, we're going to get the same results. My hope is to open the doors for new kinds of leadership.

I am an educator. I first interned in a high school classroom in 1968 and have taught almost every grade from preschool through graduate university classes over the past forty years. I have taught in private, parochial, and public schools, including twelve years with the Boston Public Schools as a teacher and headmaster. I started three schools and have overseen a few more.

This book is loaded with examples from my school and my district because this is where I spent the past twenty-five years. This is not to limit the book to a Boston audience, but to offer Boston as a case study for urban centers all over the world. Boston is a first-class city with an exceptional record, in a state that boasts one of the best educational systems in the world. Still, there are problems, which this book addresses. Later chapters branch out with stories from around the world.

To be perfectly clear, this is not a book about *teaching* entrepreneurship as part of the K–12 curriculum or how the schools can train entrepreneurial leaders. Likewise, this is not a book about how schools can make money through the practice of entrepreneurship or how enterprising people can make money in education. Rather, this is a book that examines entrepreneurial innovation operating within K–12 schooling. The literature suggests that it is very rare, but my experience tells me that it is everywhere.

There is no lack of great books for educational leaders. Jim Collins, Michael Fullan, Jim Kouzes and Barry Posner, Linda Lambert, Peter Senge, and Thomas Sergiovanni, among many others, have written compelling, motivational books that are widely read. These books inspire, rekindle the flame, build vision, sharpen skills, and otherwise increase the leadership prowess of the person in charge. However, there is very little specifically on entrepreneurial leadership within K–12 education, despite the urgent call for innovation, and there are even fewer books that recognize the innovative leadership that bubbles up from the ranks.

My goal is not to lay out the steps to promotion in the bureaucratic hierarchy of the education profession. The reader will not learn how to climb up the ladder or win the battle or beat the competition. There are some great books that address these topics, but they tend to be filled with stories of powerful people. This book is for people with powerful ideas.

The book is also written for those who are in positions of authority and worry that entrepreneurial ideas might not emerge easily in their organization, or that they might lose the entrepreneurs entirely. And to clarify, my goal is not to stir up entrepreneurial imaginations so educators will jump ship and leave schooling entirely.

The challenge here is to provide a sober examination of entrepreneurial leadership, while not smothering the entrepreneurial instinct. Frankly, a lot of entrepreneurs are not inspired by closely honed definitions; they want inspiration. Hopefully, this book achieves a balance.

## NOTES

1. Hess, F. M. (2010). *The same thing over and over: How school reformers get stuck in yesterday's ideas.* Cambridge, MA: Harvard University Press; Tyack, D. B., & Cuban, L. (1995). *Tinkering toward utopia.* New York: Corwin.

2. Fang, L. (2011, December 5). How online learning companies bought America's schools. *The Nation.*

3. Brown, R. J., & Cornwall, J. R. (Eds.). (2000). *The entrepreneurial educator.* Lanham, MD: Scarecrow Education; Hess, F. M. (2007). *Reimagining American schooling: The case for educational entrepreneurship* (Vol. 4). Washington, DC: American Enterprise Institute for Public Policy Research; Hess, F. M. (Ed.). (2008). *The future of educational entrepreneurship: Possibilities for school reform.* Cambridge, MA: Harvard Education Press; Leisey, D., & Lavaroni, C. (2000). *The educational entrepreneur: Making a difference.* San Rafael, CA: Edupreneur Press.

# INTRODUCTION

There are three main sections of this book, which mirror the purposes described in the preface. Several chapters are devoted to just describing this kind of leadership in hopes of achieving some agreement around the definition. Several more chapters look at entrepreneurial leadership for public education from an organizational standpoint and then through the eyes of the school principal and the teachers. The end of the book shifts toward entrepreneurial practices and the historic, political, and social attraction to an entrepreneurial life, which has now become worldwide.

There is a set of terms based on the French word *entrepreneur*, which are not very well defined, even in the best dictionaries. These include *entrepreneurship, entrepreneurism,* and *entrepreneurialism* as well as the title of this book, *entrepreneurial leadership*. The *entrepreneur* is a complex figure and will be thoroughly discussed in the opening chapters. However, to avoid confusing the reader, the following definitions are offered:

- *Entrepreneurialism* is a style associated with entrepreneurs, characterized by a set of traits and/or behaviors; the spirit of entrepreneurism.
- *Entrepreneurism* is the process of launching a new enterprise, which may or may not turn out to be successful.
- *Entrepreneurship* is the accomplishment of entrepreneurism; often the business or enterprise. Business schools teach entrepreneurship with success in mind.
- *Entrepreneurial leadership* is leadership that promotes entrepreneurism either directly or indirectly.

## TRANSLATIONAL RESEARCH

The approach of this book is translational, for it borrows from other disciplines—business, social science, and even physical science—in the search for answers that can stand up in the light of practice. Translational work challenges the old paradigm of applied versus basic research by breaking out of traditional domains, crossing disciplinary lines in hopes of seeing the world in new ways, and embracing new sources of data and new solutions. This new learning is emerging from unexpected quarters and informing the conception of leadership. One can do better than just create alternative routes to the top of the educational hierarchy.

As readers will discover by the end of this book, wide-ranging reading is a great way to spark innovative thinking. Readers who find interest in a particular paragraph or section will find resources for further exploration in the endnotes.

## THE OUTLINE OF THE BOOK

The subject of entrepreneurial leadership tends to invite outlandish anecdotes of renegades, and, indeed, there are some exciting and inspiring stories. While acknowledging the reality of this excitement, chapter 1 moves beyond the popular conceptions of entrepreneurship and begins to lay a scholarly foundation that would enable realistic steps toward this kind of leadership in K–12 schooling in America.

Using the approach of traditional leadership theories, a discussion of entrepreneurial traits (specific to education) is followed by a consideration of the behaviors of this kind of leader. This sequence, amply sprinkled with real stories of entrepreneurial educators, helps to bring the concept to life. (Nearly every chapter contains stories of real entrepreneurial educators. In some cases, the names have been changed or these leaders have retired, but they are all true to life.) The proper role of risk, which is inevitably associated with business entrepreneurship but often questioned in public education, is also discussed.

Chapter 2 is a serious attempt to define entrepreneurial leadership in the context of education. Rather than provide one comprehensive definition, this style of leadership is described by a series of intersecting gradients. This approach allows for a wide variety of expressions shaped by one's personal preferences and the local context. This discussion also begins crossing boundaries—a common entrepreneurial practice—into the domains of business, science, and the social sciences to better understand this kind of leadership.

Chapter 2 also presents an interesting case study of a partnership between a community college and a nearby high school, where some low-key entrepreneurial ideas were put into high gear, resulting in a frame-breaking innovation that is now spreading to other school districts and states.

Entrepreneurial leadership is popularly and inaccurately portrayed as some kind of heroic leadership where a powerful figure breaks through insurmountable obstacles to achieve success. Fortunately, this is usually far from reality, no matter what domain one considers. Real entrepreneurs, in business and the social sciences, often have a complex relationship with the institution where they work. Chapter 3 is devoted to the entrepreneurial school, which is a learning organization where the entire community is geared toward innovative thinking.

This chapter looks at leadership behaviors that are more likely to call forth innovative thinking from the ranks, an arrangement that makes clear that, in big organizations at least, the entrepreneurial thinking does not usually come from the top. The discussion of leadership practices is followed by organizational characteristics that are conducive to entrepreneurial activity. The chapter concludes with a re-analysis of the chapter 2 case study from an organizational standpoint.

Traditional school leaders, such as principals, are the focus of chapter 4. The chapter takes a round-about approach to leadership by describing the historical school reform efforts of one urban high school in Boston, Massachusetts. Looking first at the school in the 1980s and then, later, in the first decade of the twenty-first century, this chapter provides examples of leadership for an entrepreneurial organization. There are no larger-than-life heroic role models in this chapter, but rather there are stories of school improvement that won regional and national attention.

Part of turning a school into an entrepreneurial organization involves using a cultural reform strategy, which is compared here with traditional curricular and structural reform models. Finally, scalability, which is often a threat to innovation, is also discussed.

Chapter 5 returns to the teachers, who are the most overlooked of all entrepreneurial leaders. The same Boston high school is used, again, to show how three teachers led a school reform effort while administrators came and left. Other stories of individual teacher leaders are compared and contrasted, again with the purpose of dismantling the heroic vision of entrepreneurial leadership and building toward a more organic, entrepreneurial community. One little-appreciated fact is that teachers define *teacher leadership* much differently than do administrators.

Teacher leadership shows promise for entrepreneurial thinking, for it gives credence to innovation from the ranks. There are specific tips on how principals can promote entrepreneurial teacher leadership—and how teachers can emerge regardless of what their principal is doing.

The stories of chapters 2 through 5 point to a powerful springboard for entrepreneurial thinking, which is the school-community partnership, the subject of chapter 6. Community partners can include other schools, businesses, social service agencies, health clinics, and even philanthropies. They provide not only material resources, which are often scarce, but fresh perspectives and new ideas by virtue of the fact that they are, literally, outside the box of the local school.

Using Bronfenbrenner's ecological systems theory and Weick's theory of interorganizational coupling, chapter 6 uses a historical case study to analyze the causes for success or failure of entrepreneurial-type community partnerships. The chapter closes with a look at the boundary spanner, who often lives with one foot planted firmly in both partnering organizations. Many school leaders are boundary spanners, because they are always looking beyond the border of their own institution. And, interestingly enough, the border between partnering institutions is a space in which habits and traditions collide and new ideas emerge—a great place for entrepreneurial innovation.

Chapter 7 is the most translational of all the chapters, borrowing ideas and stories from economics, politics, science, and the world of art to provide a richer understanding of entrepreneurial leadership. The chapter returns to defining this style of leadership. The need for entrepreneurial leadership is reinforced with tales of disruptive innovation from the business world. The historic connections between a democratic education and entrepreneurial leadership are firmly fixed. A world tour of the grassroots innovation economy demonstrates a fundamental human drive for self-determination, again expressed in entrepreneurial thinking. Finally, a brief look at how artists think again reinforces the need for entrepreneurial leadership in education. The chapter concludes with some playful examples of how to stimulate out-of-the-box thinking in one's own place of work.

Although the reader can jump into this book at any point desired, the chapters do tend to build on one another. Case studies from earlier chapters are referenced again in later chapters. The gradients developed in chapter 2 and the organizational characteristics itemized in chapter 3 provide a structure for later chapters. For this reason, a better strategy is to read quickly from cover to cover and then return, as needed, to review information.

# ACKNOWLEDGMENTS

At the end of writing a book, one wants to thank the people who actively contributed and, even more, those who stood aside to let the book happen.

I am grateful to all the educational partners, in several schools, who demonstrated entrepreneurial leadership in their own practice and first helped me understand what I was observing. I still admire their work. I am grateful to family and friends who helped with editing.

Most of all, I am grateful for my wife Lee, the truly creative one, my three boys and their mates, and my four grandchildren. Being fully aware that they will probably never read this book makes their support even more meaningful to me.

# I

# THE CASE FOR ENTREPRENEURIAL LEADERSHIP IN EDUCATION

> The great ideas in education are never going to come from me, or frankly, from anyone else in Washington. The great ideas in education are always going to come at the local level. . . . It is going to be because of the innovation, the courage, the entrepreneurial vision of great local teachers, principals, school superintendents, school boards, that is what is going to take our country where we need to go.
> —US Secretary of Education Arne Duncan[1]

## ENTREPRENEURIAL LEADERS: RISKY BUT REQUIRED

The belief that innovation will save the American school system is widespread. Hardly a week goes by when the media does not repeat the breathless calls for innovation. For example, the topic was heralded three times in a typical issue of the nation's largest education newspaper, *Education Week*. One writer promised that the *"full talents of a nation of innovators will be released"* by the new common core curriculum standards.[2] Another proclaimed that new waivers granted under the federal No Child Left Behind legislation were going to *"unleash innovation."*[3] And a third author boasted that the recent winner of a national contest for urban school district improvement was *"a model for innovation."*[4] There seems to be nothing better than innovation in education.

These articles reveal the hope that entrepreneurial innovation will help solve the nation's education woes. The federal government selectively supports innovative ideas through the Investing in Innovation fund. Massachusetts is launching "innovation schools," and Harvard University has its own Education Innovation Laboratory.[5] The implication is that entrepreneurial energy lies just below the surface, often stifled and waiting to be released.

In reality, most people do not associate K–12 schooling with entrepreneurship.[6] The title "entrepreneur" conjures up stories of prodigies such as Bill Gates, Richard Branson, Paul Ellison, or Mark Zuckerberg—all people who quit school to make their millions. These people were creative, independent, bold risk-takers who launched new companies.

The popular perception was that schooling got in the way of their entrepreneurial dreams. Peter Thiel, the founder of PayPal and a successful hedge fund manager, offered twenty promising young students $100,000 to *drop out of school* and pursue their dreams.[7] Schools may teach entrepreneurship as a particular subject, but K–12 education is not usually considered a hothouse for entrepreneurial innovation.

This chapter explores the hopes that are pinned to innovation and uses this as a springboard to entrepreneurial leadership. What are the traits of these remarkable leaders? How can one recognize them? What do they do? Common reservations are considered. Aren't entrepreneurial leaders found in business, rather than public service? And, especially, what is the place of risk in public education?


## WHY ALL THE INTEREST IN INNOVATION?

There is an increasing appreciation that education is the key to economic security. Unlike the nineteenth century, when a few years of schooling were sufficient for most occupations, today many American industries want their workers with more than a high school diploma. A college education is increasingly perceived to be the standard for success.

At the same time, there is an overwhelming perception that the American K–12 public school system is failing. Despite new education legislation and massive funding, there is convincing evidence that our students overall cannot compete with other nations. While our top students are competitive, there is a troubling achievement gap with many underperforming students left behind. In both big cities and outlying rural districts, far too many students are stuck in schools with low test scores and high dropout rates. Furthermore, parents watch in dismay as traditional staples of a well-rounded public education, such as the arts, civics, and physical education programs, wither.

As long as education is increasingly valued and available evidence indicates that current policies and practices are not meeting the demand, then there will be a need for innovation in education.

Many educational innovations have been driven by new sources outside the traditional K–12 school system. The public, stirred up to find good schools, began to seek alternatives, which led to an explosion of home schools, parochial schools, private schools, and online learning. Rightfully or not, publicly funded K–12 schooling was increasingly seen as a monopoly to be challenged with aggressive competition.

Over thirty years ago, the business community also began to engage with K–12 schooling. Historically, businesses marketed to the *needs* of schools, but after 1980, they began to get more directly engaged with the *work* of schools, looking more critically at academic standards, accountability, and leadership practices. Today, the business community is looking *beyond* traditional schooling in hopes that new enterprises, such as charter management organizations, online learning opportunities, and directive business partnerships, can lead education reform.

The engagement of the business world with public education is hotly debated with passionate voices on both sides. Businesses have a profit-making motive, which is at odds with the public purposes of K–12 schooling. Detractors decry the competitive nature of the business world, with winners and losers, which is incompatible with the democratic purposes of schooling. On the other hand, schools all over the nation have been valuably supported by capitalistic enterprises.[8] And, there is no denying that businesses are more oriented toward innovation than most schools. Business guru Peter Senge pointed out:

> Gradually, I came to realize why business is the locus of innovation in an open society. Despite whatever hold past thinking may have on the business mind, business has a freedom to experiment missing in the public sector and, often, in nonprofit organizations.[9]

This book takes the position that innovation is an indispensable part of school improvement, requiring new forms of leadership and, specifically, entrepreneurial leadership. Innovation and entrepreneurial leadership go hand-in-hand. A closer consideration of both concepts is needed.

## WHAT DOES INNOVATION MEAN?

Innovation is confusing because there is a spectrum of meanings. The *Oxford English Dictionary* defines innovation in at least three ways.[10]

The word *innovation* can refer to a new thing, as in this definition: "A change made in the nature or fashion of anything; something newly introduced; a novel practice, method, etc." Here, the innovation is an invention, such as the printing press or a cell phone. Secondly, the word *innovation* can describe a *process*, such as the "action of innovating; the introduction of novelties." As a result, some innovations might be new to an organization, even though they have been around for a while. And, finally, the word *innovation* can have a *commercial* meaning, which is "the action of introducing a new product into the market." Harvard scholar Rosabeth Moss Kanter, who has studied business entrepreneurship for over thirty years, summarized these definitions when she wrote, "Innovation is the generation, acceptance, and implementation of new ideas, processes, products, or services."[11]

Innovation means change, and that's where a lot of the resistance originates. One scholar, who writes frequently on the topic, was asked to define the term. He replied, "That's a difficult question. But one thing is for sure: If you're not pissing someone off, it's probably not innovation." He went on to add, "I like this response because, if it doesn't end the conversation, it usually shifts it from definitions to dynamics—which is what innovation is all about, after all."[12] Entrepreneurs, of course, lose patience splitting hairs over definitions and want to get on to results.

As chapter 2 will explain, the concept of entrepreneurship has multiple meanings as well, which match the spectrum for innovation. Some entrepreneurs live at the *invention* end of the spectrum and some live at the *commercial* end of the spectrum. These different connotations are important but confusing. For example, some school leaders are remarkably innovative and may even invent new school forms. Other leaders are entrepreneurial, not because they are *personally* inventive, but because they foster innovation in others. These leaders surround themselves with innovation.

Deborah Meier earned her national reputation as the founder and director of Central Park East, an alternative elementary school in New York City, which many consider the beginning of the small schools movement in public education.[13] Meier was inspired and assisted by Ted Sizer, who was the founder of the Coalition of Essential Schools, which has grown to a national network of over six hundred public schools.[14] Eric Swarz is the co-founder and CEO of Citizen Schools, which partners with middle schools in low-income neighborhoods to enrich students' lives with an expanded learning day.[15] These people are game-changing, entrepreneurial leaders who are famous for their innovative thinking.

Other school leaders are not inventive, but they can spot a good idea when they see it and move it into implementation. Maybe they read about the idea in an article or picked it up on a visit to another school or maybe a teacher came up with the idea. The point is that someone recognized the worth of the idea and moved on the implementation of the idea. Both kinds of leaders are entrepreneurial leaders.

Mike Sabin became principal of the Edwards Middle School in Charlestown, Massachusetts, when the school was struggling academically and up for possible closure. Mike replaced 50 percent of the teachers and gave the new faculty common planning time, lengthened class periods, and reduced class sizes. He brought in student teachers to increase the adult/student ratio. Still, the year-end test results were discouraging and the school did not make adequate yearly progress under the federal guidelines for school improvement.[16] Mike then heard about state funds for an extended learning day and won a grant, which he used to lengthen the school day in partnership with Citizens Schools. The combination of time and services proved effective for student success. Today, Edwards is one of Boston's highest performing middle schools. The head of Citizen Schools boasted, "Over the course of four years, the school eliminated the achievement gap for students in math and erased eighty percent of the state gap on literacy and science standardized tests."[17]

## WHAT IS ENTREPRENEURIAL LEADERSHIP?

The entrepreneurial leader begins with a question—*how can we do this better?*—and then turns the innovative ideas into policies, programs, and enterprises, which have intellectual, social, and/or economic value. The entrepreneurial leader is the person who ensures that the process moves forward, either personally or by means of the organization. As this book will demonstrate, in some cases the leader may not be very entrepreneurial, but the leader identifies with the process. Entrepreneurism is a priority.

This definition is appealing for several reasons. The emphasis is on the creation of value, and public schooling is indisputably an ethical undertaking. Educators share, with parents, responsibility for the upbringing of children. The vulnerability of young minds implies moral responsibility. Every day, they make choices for children, in terms of curriculum, pedagogy, and guidance, which reflect personal values and moral standards. For this reason, the emphasis on value creation is paramount for this book. Any entrepreneurial activity that ultimately

robs children of resources—because it is overly risky or self-serving—is
not worth promoting.

The definition of entrepreneurial leadership emphasizes value creation, which could be intellectual, social, and/or economic. When a middle school math teacher discovers an innovative way to help students
make the cognitive leap from concrete arithmetic to abstract algebra,
that is entrepreneurial leadership with intellectual value creation.
When high schoolers work together on a protocol for conflict mediation
in their school, they are exercising entrepreneurial leadership with social value.

Not all entrepreneurs pursue profits. For some, other values are
paramount, such as the education of children, or neighborhood improvement or civic engagement. These are called social entrepreneurs
to distinguish them from economic or business entrepreneurs. Chapter
2 will revisit this term. However, many believe that the traits and behaviors of both kinds of entrepreneurs are similar.

Lynn Gatto was an entrepreneurial teacher working with low-income students in an urban elementary school in upstate New York.
Looking for hands-on activities for her social studies course in state
geography, she read about using cookie cutters shaped like the United
States. With a small grant, she invented and produced her own cookie
cutter in the shape of New York state. Her students used some of the
grant money to create a teacher's guide on how to use the cookie cutter
in class activities. Later, with help from a guest speaker, the students
started a business based on the cookie cutters and the guides and used
the profits for more classroom projects.[18] This was entrepreneurial
leadership that generated intellectual, social, and economic value.

Leadership is a valuable commodity in every endeavor, whether education or otherwise, so the topic has generated intense study for over
one hundred years. The theories of leadership have evolved, and each
stage offers something to further one's understanding of specifically
entrepreneurial leadership. In the beginning, researchers wanted to
identify the distinguishing marks of leaders so they could better spot
up-and-coming leaders. However, this approach implied that leaders
were born with these traits. Later researchers were more interested in
what leaders do, which might suggest ways in which anyone could become a better leader. Both theories are considered here.

Chapter 2 compares entrepreneurial leadership with other leadership styles, such as charismatic, transformational, and democratic leaders. In recent years, the context in which leadership is exercised, and
the interaction between leaders and their environment, has been the
focus of investigation, leading to recent interest in contingency theory,

situated leadership theory, and, most recently, a distributed theory of leadership.[19] These are addressed in chapters 2 and 3.

## ENTREPRENEURIAL LEADERSHIP TRAITS

Trait theory speculates that exemplary leadership derives from a set of inborn personality characteristics. The business world has, understandably, studied successful entrepreneurs intensively in hopes of identifying characteristic traits and better recognizing future entrepreneurs for business leadership or venture capital investment. To a much lesser extent, the traits of entrepreneurial educational leaders, both within and around K–12 education, have been explored also. While no list of traits is absolutely definitive, the traits most often delineated clarify this kind of leadership.

Entrepreneurial leaders are, above all things, characterized by how they group a vexing problem and an innovative idea, which they embrace with a passion that borders on obsession. They are imaginative, creative people who fulfill the stereotype of leaders who "think outside the box." They are attracted to new ideas. They look and listen for them. They love the exploration, the development, the implementation, the new territory. They generate ideas. They collect ideas. Sometimes, their idea is not original, but borrowed, for entrepreneurs can be great opportunists, and they embrace it as if it were their own.[20] They are unusually experimental with a willingness to try every conceivable means to achieve success. Both the innovative idea and the final route to successful implementation can be either invented or borrowed. The main thing is the inspiration.

For entrepreneurial leaders, the idea becomes almost central to their identity, which is actualized through successful implementation. These people take ownership—of the problem, the solution, and the implementation—and in this their leadership is most evident.[21] They take initiative and tend to be real go-getters.[22] These leaders can appear, at times, to have enormous egos, brimming with self-confidence, but this is limited to the realm of their idea. Often, they are quite charismatic, with an ability to share their dream with infectious enthusiasm, but this is not always the case.

One thing is clear: they love what they do. Joi Ito, the director of the MIT Media Center, pointed out,

> When people talk about innovation as if it were a government or corporate or academic thing, I think they're missing a huge reason

why people do innovative things. In fact, a lot of us do things for the love of it.[23]

Entrepreneurial thinkers can "smell" the challenge, adventure, discovery, and imminent satisfaction.

More importantly, entrepreneurial leaders are relentless in their pursuit of a particular idea or dream.[24] They are decisive people, "making decisions quickly alone or with modest amounts of advice"—but again, this is limited to their interest area.[25] Otherwise, they can appear unengaged or disinterested. There is efficiency in their approach; the problem and the solution are all-consuming and other tasks and people will take a backseat.

Researchers note that entrepreneurial people often have a high tolerance for ambiguity. Whether facing scant resources, conflicting evidence, or questionable support, they are comfortable in the pursuit of their idea. For them, the one thing that is not ambiguous is the idea that there is a solution to a pressing problem.

At times, the singular focus on and relentless pursuit of their vision can make them appear competitively aggressive.[26] Entrepreneurial educators are ambitious, not in pursuit of money but as in wanting to solve a puzzle. They are tenacious and often demonstrate great perseverance through multiple setbacks.[27] They are stubbornly persistent. Deborah Meier, for example, felt she lacked many of the character traits of the entrepreneur, but she was persistent. She explained, "I wasn't an innovator, but stubbornly just trying to put into practice what I liked best about my own upbringing and schooling."[28]

Unlike other kinds of leaders, entrepreneurial leaders are more independent, appearing oblivious to obstacles and naysayers. In their autonomy, they are unswayed by public opinion. They can forge ahead with an idea in the face of universal skepticism. For this reason, they are often characterized as courageous reformers, bold in the face of opposition.[29] Certainly, they are not afraid of a fight.[30] Some have called them rebels or the "James Deans" of the educational world.[31] One notable entrepreneurial superintendent, when asked what book he kept by his bedside, referenced *First, Break All the Rules: What the World's Greatest Managers Do Differently* by Marcus Buckingham and Curt Coffman.[32] They can definitely have a chip on their shoulders related to their impatience with distractions or interference from controlling organizations.[33]

Psychologists say these leaders have a high internal locus of control, which means they tend to believe that they are in control of their destiny.[34] In contrast, people with a high external locus of control tend to attribute life's outcomes to outside factors beyond their control. Entrepreneurial leaders like to be in control.[35] Many entrepreneurs long to work for themselves even if it means loss of income and greater risk. They often tend to micromanage their pet projects.

Despite their autonomy, these entrepreneurial leaders are not loners; they understand that alliances are essential for success. They are pragmatic in their approach to relationships, attending to those who will bolster their idea and ignoring those who are not relevant. They are pragmatic in their fights; they pick their battles carefully.[36] They are also pragmatic in their experimentation with successful pathways to implementation,[37] being willing to try almost "every means imaginable to make it happen."[38] In a sense, the end justifies the means, which is one reason people often look skeptically at this kind of leadership.

The one other trait that is most often associated with entrepreneurial leaders is that they are risk-tolerant. At whatever stage, whether going it alone, experimenting with alternative solutions, or facing down opposition, they are comfortable taking risks. Given their work with vulnerable children and scarce resources, some question whether this kind of leadership belongs in public education, a concern that is addressed later in this chapter. On a positive note, their adventuresome spirit, which is always experimenting and exploring new ideas, makes them lifelong learners.

The definition of entrepreneurial leadership offered earlier emphasized value creation. It's not enough just to have innovative ideas. The term "entrepreneur" is an *ex post* concept, meaning that it is calculated retrospectively.[39] Entrepreneurs do not earn the title until they have had one strong success—and they might have many failures preceding this. Similar to other common *ex post* terms, such as "artist" or "champion," they are usually identified by their results. For this reason, trait theory falls short. Someone might have all the entrepreneurial traits, but lacking that one success, he is still not an entrepreneur. Consequently, scholars also look at what they do and not just what they appear to be.

## ENTREPRENEURIAL BEHAVIORS

Process theory predicates that leadership behaviors can be learned, in contrast to trait theory. No doubt, there is some truth to both approaches. There would be little sense in having courses in entrepreneurship in every business school in America if the behaviors could not be learned. Some of what entrepreneurs do is easily derived from their characteristic traits.

There is no shortage of problems in public education; some come to the school along with the children and others result from school dysfunction. As a result, school leaders can sometimes become jaded and unresponsive to the most obvious needs around them. Entrepreneurial leaders have a different perspective; where others see problems in the school, they see opportunities.[40] A good problem is a challenge, an invitation to new learning and potential innovation.

Some have called these leaders *gap fillers* because of their uncanny ability to spot a need and provide a solution.[41] While the literature in education often speaks of an achievement gap, there are also countless gaps in the day-to-day functioning of a school that reflect the poor allocation of resources, unrecognized deficiencies, or shifting priorities. Entrepreneurial leaders spot the mission gaps and delivery gaps and look for innovative solutions.

Lynn Gatto is a good example. She began her career as a special education teacher. She discovered that the parents of her students had a poor understanding of their child's disability, so she used a $500 grant to create an educational videotape. The video taught parents about learning disabilities, with suggestions for how they could work with their teachers and help their children at home. For Lynn, the problem was just an interesting opportunity.[42]

Entrepreneurial leaders are constantly alert to opportunities.[43] The opportunity could be a problem that begs for a solution, thus launching the wheels of innovation, or it could be a good idea that pops up in an educational journal or a conversation with a colleague. Sometimes, the good idea brings to light a previously unrecognized or unaddressed problem.

For example, as an elementary school teacher, Lynn Gatto was browsing the vendor exhibits at a national science teachers convention and spotted a science curriculum that she really liked. She was disappointed to find that the curriculum was not written for elementary students, and, after exploring the gap, she was encouraged by the owner of the company to write the expanded curriculum herself. She signed a contract, which honored her insistence on units that were project based and allowed ample room for teacher modification, and then developed nine science kits. She then went on to offer training workshops in support of the new, successful curriculum.[44]

Being alert to opportunities means taking the time to consider other people's ideas.[45] Some leaders feel a need to have all the answers, but successful leaders know from experience that, while they have their own narrow band of expertise, they are incapable of having the solution to every problem. Entrepreneurial leaders listen, not just to build relationships or encourage collegiality, but because they are on the hunt for better ideas. They listen selectively.

These leaders are observant. They notice what's going on around them, especially when it looks promising, just as Lynn Gatto did in the exhibit hall. They dig in and ask questions. They are researchers. Asking questions is a developed art. Every researcher can attest to the fact that in the beginning the questions are hard to generate and few in number, but over time, they proliferate and pile up. Eventually, asking questions is a lifestyle. The entrepreneur is always asking, "How can we do this better?" and looking for new solutions.[46] They must sift among the many possibilities and weigh which ones are worth pursuing.

Entrepreneurial leaders practice associational thinking, which means they put incongruous things together in their mind.[47] Their restlessness leads them across disciplines and into new domains of knowledge. They collect bits and pieces of ideas, which emerge over time in a creative solution. In this respect, they are like artists. This knack for cross-disciplinary thinking is taken up more fully in chapter 7.

As leaders, these entrepreneurial individuals venture out; they take initiative and act on their ideas.[48] Kouzes and Posner, in their groundbreaking study of great leaders, wrote that "none of the individuals in our study sat idly by waiting for fate to smile upon them."[49] Venturing out is not unique to entrepreneurial leadership; all leaders have to stick their neck out, but it's worth emphasizing that entrepreneurial leaders are not laboratory dreamers. Furthermore, they are less likely to delegate the problem to someone else. They act on their ideas. Inevitably, they challenge the status quo since that is the nature of innovation. Again, Kouzes and Posner wrote, "Not one person claimed to have achieved a personal best by keeping things the same. All leaders challenge the process."[50]

These leaders often sink or swim based on their ability to communicate a compelling vision that inspires others, builds alliances, and secures resources.[51] Certainly, the charismatic personality is helpful at this point, but sheer determination accompanied by deeply held beliefs can accomplish the same, as Deborah Meier demonstrated.[52] Entrepreneurial leaders should be able to communicate their idea in a compelling way in thirty seconds or less—the classic elevator speech. This only happens when the values are crystal clear and the core components carefully composed.

Entrepreneurial leaders take risks, but they are not reckless. Instead, they take calculated risks, weighing the risk of "missing the boat" versus "sinking the boat."[53] They are more likely to take risks when they believe they can influence the outcome.[54] Entrepreneurial leaders have been found to have a high sense of self-efficacy in the areas of innovativeness and risk-taking.[55] They understand that the greatest risk in life is not taking one at all. Sometimes, these leaders will minimize the risks by running a pilot project, which allows them to try out the idea on a reduced scale. Pilot projects are easier to track, which facilitates learning, and they minimize the damage in the event of failure.

A lack of resources does not intimidate entrepreneurial leaders. The opportunity is everything; they know resources will follow. Former professor of business administration at the Harvard Business School Howard Stevenson defined entrepreneurship as "the pursuit of opportunity beyond the tangible resources that you currently control."[56] To paraphrase Robert Browning, their reach exceeds their grasp.[57]

These leaders are resource scavengers. They gather resources, whether from inside the organization or outside, and they think creatively about how to allocate scarce resources for targeted impact. Schools never have enough money, supplies, time, and people, but entrepreneurial leaders think strategically about how to line resources up to accomplish their goal.

Ralph Spezio was a new principal in a troubled inner city elementary school who quickly realized that his students were already behind their suburban counterparts when they entered his school in kindergarten. Nothing short of an early childhood learning center would address the need, but the district was unsupportive in light of the lack of building space. With this resource challenge, Spezio approached a major city corporation and found funding for a new wing on his school. He partnered with the nearby vocational school and had students build the frame structures. Meanwhile, he researched early childhood learning programs and selected the Montessori model for his new preschool. At each step, he partnered with community agencies to maximize his resources. In the end, he had a program which allowed his students to start school years in advance, an important step toward academic success.[58]

Finding needed resources is one skill; steering the entrepreneurial project through all the obstacles and hurdles is a related skill. Sometimes, the best-funded projects end up going nowhere because of organizational hurdles. This is the topic of chapter 3, which is addressed both to school leaders and those who are in a position to lower the hurdles.

The entrepreneurial leader must learn how to spot the potential obstacles and take steps in advance to overcome or circumvent them. Sometimes, just ignoring the organizational regulations is sufficient. Knowing full well that central administration is not likely to support some new innovation, more than one entrepreneurial principal has embraced this motto: "Better to ask forgiveness later than permission beforehand." This requires some boldness. Again, recommended reading might be *First, Break All the Rules: What the World's Great Managers Do Differently*.[59] These leaders are fence-jumpers. They're not bothered by hurdles. They are escape artists.

As noted previously, entrepreneurial leaders are "on the hunt" for new ideas and better solutions. They scrounge for resources to forward their vision. All this implies that they are constantly networking, despite their independent nature. As Ralph Spezio demonstrated, they build partnerships and coalitions, not just within their own professional circle but across public, private, and non-profit sectors. Other people and partnering organizations can provide encouragement, material resources, personnel support, or a location for a field test. Chapter 6 will explore this more deeply.

Entrepreneurs are hands-on leaders who pay attention to important details and delegate those things they consider unimportant. For example, they may spend a lot of time creating a business plan, but count on someone else to write it up for reporting purposes. They micromanage and monitor everything.[60] Entrepreneurial leaders are data hounds. They want to find out what is working and what is not; data can help them make mid-stream adjustments if necessary. Giving up is not easy for an entrepreneur, but given their pragmatic nature, they are willing to cut their losses and try something else when the data are not encouraging. Entrepreneurs are not wedded to one idea, but to a satisfactory, sustainable solution. In the long run, they are constantly improving, strengthening, and broadening the vision.

David Bornstein, who has written extensively on social entrepreneurs, sums up the behaviors of these leaders in this way:

> An important social change frequently begins with a single entrepreneurial author: one obsessive individual who sees a problem and envisions a new solution, who takes the initiative to act on that vision, who gathers resources and builds organizations to protect and market that vision, who provides the energy and sustained focus to overcome the inevitable resistance, and who—decade after decade— keeps improving, strengthening, and broadening that vision until what was once a marginal idea has become a new norm.[61]

These leaders rarely give in to discouragement. Everyone fails at some point, but entrepreneurial leaders learn from their failures, get up, and start again. One never finds an entrepreneur who hasn't experienced a major setback; in this respect they are unremarkable. What distinguishes entrepreneurs is that they spring back. This might be the defining characteristic, more than any other indicator.

Sometimes, people assume that entrepreneurial leadership means running a school like a business. One author wrote that the entrepreneurial leader "applies market principles to schools . . . encouraging competition" and "providing incentives for winning and disincentives for losing."[62] Teachers, parents, and students would find this unattractive. Entrepreneurial school leaders are not businessmen in school clothing. They are more like artists who draw outside the lines.

## WHY AREN'T THERE MORE ENTREPRENEURIAL LEADERS IN EDUCATION?

Some will question this constant drumbeat for innovation. Veteran teachers sometimes roll their eyes at the latest innovation, for they have seen them come and go for years. Parents and educators often envision the school as the one place where traditions are cherished and "progress" is held at bay. From sports to school proms to graduation ceremonies, people expect their schools to be largely as they were when they attended as children. This is the American way, preserved in their schools more than any other place. Americans want their schools to be a safe haven for children where they are protected from reckless innovations.

Too often, however, children struggle with long periods of seat work devoted to reading, writing, and wrestling with abstract ideas with little opportunity to really act out on those ideas. Student engagement is a national problem, which only grows as students progress through school.[63] When schools fall short on real-world authenticity, neglecting cooperative learning strategies, project-based learning, service learning, and technological applications, they fail the expectations of young people who are growing up in the twenty-first century. Students expect relevance, and "innovation is the only insurance against irrelevance."[64]

In 1997 two management scholars by the names of Heifetz and Laurie shook up the business world with a short article on adaptive change.[65] Organizations face many challenges for which the solution is obvious to everyone. In a school, for example, if the classrooms are cold or textbooks are lacking, everyone knows what to do. Repairing a heating system or finding funds for textbooks can be difficult, but these kinds of challenges do not require new learning as much as hard work. These are technical challenges. However, there are other challenges— adaptive challenges—for which the answers are not so obvious. The world of public education is full of adaptive challenges, such as the achievement gap, where white students often score better on standardized tests than students of color. The focus today on designing evaluations for effective teaching is another adaptive challenge because no one is exactly sure what effective teaching looks like.

Adaptive challenges require experimentation, risk-taking, new learning, and change—terms which bring us back to innovation. This is worth repeating: as long as education is increasingly valued and available evidence indicates that current policy and practice is not meeting the demand, then there will be a need for innovation in education. And, for that, one needs entrepreneurial leaders in the classroom and in the administrative offices.

The cautious approach to education reduces the professional work of K–12 teachers and administrators to technical expertise, with insufficient attention to innovative thinking and adaptive learning. The focus is on data-driven decision-making in the main office and test preparation in the classroom is not conducive to flights of imagination and out-of-the-box thinking. There are countless schools which list on their mission statement that they intend "to produce lifelong learners," but they fail to model the thing that they prize. Educators are often cautious, tradition bound, threatened by accountability, and afraid of new ideas.

This fear of the unexpected is not conducive to creating lifelong learners. Contrast the scripted curricula and tight accountability schedules of most schools today with these words from Joi Ito of the MIT Media lab, an institution which is dedicated to innovation:

> You need to give up the idea of control and be confident in your ability to pull things together as you go. . . . Drowning in ten feet of water isn't any different than drowning in a million feet. And if you can swim, it doesn't matter how deep the ocean is. At some level, once you realize you're in water that's too deep to stand, you have to have a very different approach, which is basically: Plans don't work, mapping doesn't work. You need a compass and a trajectory and some values to figure it out as you go along.[66]

While lesson plans are valuable, teachers who have watched their plans unravel will recognize the truth of these words. If schools do not teach their children to run, to swim, and to fly in their imaginations, those students will never fall in love with lifelong learning.

Despite the need for entrepreneurial leaders, their distinguishing traits can make them anathema to veteran educators. In this era of standards where conformity is rewarded, who is interested in teachers who think outside the box? Under strict accountability regimens, what superintendent wants to hire a James Dean principal who believes rules are made to be broken?

Researchers in California scoured the public schools for entrepreneurial leadership, too often finding that "the very people who might make some important changes left the schools for employment in other, often related, fields."[67] Equally discouraging was their report that they could not find a single district that had a program in place to identify, encourage, and support entrepreneurially minded leaders.

Entrepreneurial leadership may appear to be an endangered species inside the public K–12 education system, but this same kind of leadership flourishes in the business world of education, which includes all the companies that supply textbooks and curricular materials, classroom supplies, performance assessments, academic tutoring, professional development programs, and all the other things that are required in every school. This world is expanding, as entrepreneurs eye an enormous customer base and a trillion-dollar education budget.

## THE PLACE FOR RISK IN PUBLIC EDUCATION

In the business world, the risk-tolerant and opportunistic behavior of entrepreneurs can have serious consequences including job loss, bankruptcy, and lawsuits, accompanied by broken relationships, loss of pride, and ruined reputation. Who wants this in the public school classroom? The risk-taking nature of entrepreneurial leaders is troubling in public education in light of the vulnerable young minds who sit in US schools. This issue, more than any other, distinguishes public service from the fast and furious world of business. Is risk-taking even appropriate when working with children?

Risk-taking is fundamental to education. Children cannot learn without taking risks. They cannot explore new knowledge, test new ideas, try out new roles, or question or challenge established dogmas without venturing into the unknown and becoming vulnerable. Learning means risking exposure, failure, or even loss. For this reason, risk-taking should be a guiding theme in education, instead of something that draws resistance and rebuke for those who dare to rock the boat.

Interestingly, the role of risk in the learning process is well appreciated in the creative arts. An art teacher was taking a graduate class in educational leadership and was surprised to discover the quandary over risk-taking in education. She said, "Risk-taking is status quo in my world. Every rubric we use to evaluate students' artwork has risk written in as an invariable element."[68] In essence, she said, modern art is distinguished by the risk taken in departing from the traditional. And yet, in the national rush to improve student achievement test scores in math, science, and English, the creative arts have often been downgraded or eliminated in school curricula. As a result, educators have grown unfamiliar with the proper role of risk.

Roland Barth, a former teacher, school principal, and founder of the Principal Center at Harvard University once wrote,

> There is growth and learning in failure. There is no growth and no learning in fear of failure. If you take away a person's right to fail, you take away her right to succeed. [69]

Esther Dyson is an entrepreneur, philanthropist, and angel investor who also trained for a visit to the International Space Station. Clearly, she understands risk! She offered the following advice:

> So how do you encourage useful innovation? By doing two things. One, you have to promote risk taking—be open to experimentation and philosophical about things that go wrong. My motto is, "Always make new mistakes." There's no shame in making a mistake. But then learn from it and don't make the same one again. Everything I've learned, I've learned by making mistakes. [70]

Every good classroom teacher understands that the adventure of learning is a risk-taking journey from the known to the unknown. For this reason, a better approach is not to figure out how to eliminate risks, but how to create safety nets so that everyone involved in education, whether children, teachers, or leaders, can dare to experiment, challenge the process, pursue new ideas, and learn from the mistakes.

Michael Fung, a former high school principal, was an instructional leader with high expectations. He spent hours in the classroom with his new teachers and wrote long evaluations with lots of feedback. To his dismay, some promising new teachers just withered under the attention and quit. In their mind, the risk of failure was too high. Instead of curtailing his evaluations, Fung invented "forgiveness sticks" and gave three to each new teacher. Each stick had the teacher's name and the date on which he or she was hired. The forgiveness sticks were a safety net for intimidated teachers. They could stumble without fear, knowing that all they had to do was hand a forgiveness stick to Michael. As a result, they were able to relax and return to the experimentation that is fundamental to growth and improvement. [71]

## CONCLUSION

A book on entrepreneurial leadership is problematic for several reasons. The heroic interpretation of leadership has long been discounted, but these leaders do seem to have extraordinary traits. Some of their behaviors raise questions as well about the role of risk in education. The association of entrepreneurial leadership with the world of business, where the profit motive is dominant, raises other concerns.

This chapter began by defining the concept of innovation, followed by reasons for the high demand for innovation in education at this time. As long as education is valued and the available evidence indicates that current practices are not meeting the demand, then there will be a need for innovation in education. Innovation calls for entrepreneurial leadership, which is characterized by a distinctive list of traits and behaviors. For a variety of reasons, entrepreneurial leadership is not easily discovered in the public and private K–12 schools of America.

Entrepreneurial leaders succeed, in part, because they are willing to take risks and learn from their failures and successes. As lifelong learners, all educators should be comfortable taking risks and venturing into the unknown. One way to restore the excitement of learning is to create safety nets.

## NOTES

1. King, J. (2010, August 9). Interview with Education Secretary Arne Duncan. *Real Clear Politics,* para. 20–21.

2. Wiggins, G. (2011, September 28). The common-core math standards: They don't add up. *Education Week, 31,* 22.

3. Attributed to a "senior administration official" by Klein, A. (2011, September 22). Obama administration sets rules for NCLB waivers, para. 3. Retrieved from http://blogs.edweek.org/edweek/campaign-k-12/2011/09/obama_administration_sets_rule.html.

4. Samuels, C. A. (2011). Charlotte-Mecklenburg wins Broad Prize. *Education Week, 31*(5), para. 2. Retrieved from http://www.edweek.org/ew/articles/2011/09/20/05broad.h31.html.

5. On the Investing in Education fund, see http://www2.ed.gov/programs/innovation/index.html; for MA innovation schools, see http://www.mass.gov/edu/innovation-schools.html; and for Harvard program, see http://www.edlabs.harvard.edu/.

6. For just one example, M. Ellsberg asks a provocative question in his article titled "Will dropouts save America?" (2011, October 22), *The New York Times.*

7. Ironically, Thiel completed both college and graduate school. Associated Press. (2011, June 8). Mogul pays bright minds not to go to college. *Education Week, 30,* 5.

8. The school in which I served is an excellent example, where the TJX Companies, Verizon Corporation, and Sovereign Bank were invaluable partners.

9. Senge, P. (2006). *The fifth dimension: The art and practice of the learning organization* (p. 15). New York: Doubleday.

10. *Oxford English Dictionary.* (2010). New York: Oxford University Press.

11. Kanter, R. M. (1983). *The change masters: Innovation and entrepreneurship in the American corporation* (p. 20). New York: Simon & Schuster, Inc.

12. Auerswald, P. (2012, May 4). If you're not pissing someone off, you're probably not innovating, para. 1–2. Retrieved from http://blogs.hbr.org/cs/2012/05/if_youre_not_pissing_someone_o.html.

13. Meier, D. (2012a). About me. Retrieved September 7, 2012, from http://deborahmeier.com/about/.

14. A common vision. (2012). Retrieved September 7, 2012, from http://www.essentialschools.org/network.

15. What we do. (2012). Retrieved September 7, 2012, from http://www.citizenschools.org/.

16. Bernier, K. C. (2008). *Expanding learning time: How the Edwards Middle School in Boston partnered with Citizen Schools to transform the learning day* (p. 32). Boston, MA: Citizen Schools.

17. Swarz, E. (2012, May 14). We need a longer school day, para. 8. Retrieved September 7, 2012, from http://www.timetosucceed.com/2012/05/14/we-need-a-longer-school-day/.

18. Vitagliano, R., & Khan, S. (2007). *Teacher as social entrepreneur: Practices of an innovative and resourceful urban elementary school teacher.* Paper presented at the annual meeting of the American Educational Research Association, Chicago, IL.

19. Spillane, J. (2006). *Distributed leadership.* San Francisco, CA: Jossey-Bass; Spillane, J., Halverson, R., & Diamond, J. (2004). Towards a theory of leadership practice: A distributed perspective. *Journal of Curriculum Studies, 36*(1), 3–34.

20. Gladwell, M. (2010). The sure thing: How entrepreneurs really succeed. *New Yorker, 86*(3), 24–29; Hentschke, G., & Caldwell, B. J. (2005). Entrepreneurial leadership. In B. Davies (Ed.), *The essentials of school leadership* (pp. 145–159). Thousand Oaks, CA: Corwin Press.

21. Williams, J. (2006). Breaking the mold: How do school entrepreneurs create change? *Education Next, 6*(2), 42–49.

22. Vitagliano, R., & Khan, S.

23. Jannot, M. (2012). Making gadgets great. *Popular Science,* para. 21. Retrieved January 26, 2013, from http://www.popsci.com/bown/2011/innovator/making-gadgets-great.

24. Hentschke, G., & Caldwell, B. J. (2005). Entrepreneurial leadership. In B. Davies (Ed.), *The essentials of school leadership* (pp. 145–159). Thousand Oaks, CA: Corwin Press.

25. Hentschke, G., & Caldwell, B. J., 151.

26. Eyal, O., & Kark, R. (2004). How do transformational leaders transform organizations? A study of the relationship between leadership and entrepreneurship. *Leadership and Policy in Schools, 3*(3), 211–235.

27. Hentschke, G., & Caldwell, B. J.

28. Meier, D. (2012b, September 13). On Diane and Mission Hill, para. 3. Retrieved from http://blogs.edweek.org/edweek/Bridging-Differences/2012/09/dear_diane_i_shall_miss.html

29. Hentschke, G., & Caldwell, B. J.

30. Williams, J.

31. Hess, F. M. (Ed.). (2006). *Educational entrepreneurship: Realities, challenges, possibilities*. Cambridge, MA: Harvard Education Press; Williams, J.

32. Goldman, J. P. (2005). Charting Yakima on a far-reaching roadmap. *School Administrator, 62*(7), 51. The Buckingham/Coffman book was published by Simon &Schuster in 1999.

33. Williams, J.

34. Reimers-Hild, C., King, J. W., Foste, J. E., Fritz, S. M., Waller, S. S., & Wheeler, D. W. (2005). A framework for the "entrepreneurial" learner of the 21st century. *Online Journal of Distance Learning Administration, 8*(2).

35. Hentschke, G., & Caldwell, B. J.

36. Williams, J.

37. Hentschke, G., & Caldwell, B. J.

38. Williams, J., para. 34.

39. Martin, R. L., & Osberg, S. (2007). Social entrepreneurship: The case for definition. *Stanford Social Innovation Review, 5*(2), 28–39.

40. Hentschke, G., & Caldwell, B. J.

41. Boyett, I., & Finlay, D. (1993). The emergence of the educational entrepreneur. *Long Range Planning, 26*(3), 114–122.

42. Vitagliano, R., & Khan, S.

43. Borasi, R., & Ames, M. (2007). *Developing more effective academic leaders: Lessons learned from the case study of an entrepreneurial dean*. Paper presented at the annual meeting of the American Educational Research Association, Chicago, IL.

44. Vitagliano, R., & Khan, S.

45. Borasi, R., & Ames, M.

46. Alternatively, Warren Berger—author of *A More Beautiful Question* (2013) from Bloomsbury—asks this question: "How might we….?" Berger, W. (2012, September 12). The secret phrase top innovators use. Retrieved from http://blogs.hbr.org/cs/2012/09/the_secret_phrase_top_innovato.html.

47. Christensen, C. M., Gregersen, H. B., & Dyer, J. H. (2011). The innovator's DNA: Mastering the five skills of disruptive innovators. *Harvard Business School Press Books*, 304; Upbin, B. (2011). The five habits of highly innovative

leaders. *Forbes*. Retrieved from http://www.forbes.com/sites/bruceupbin/2011/07/20/the-five-habits-of-highly-innovative-leaders/.

48. Hentschke, G., & Caldwell, B. J.

49. Kouzes, J. M., & Posner, B. Z. (2008). *The leadership challenge* (4th ed., p. 18). San Francisco: Jossey-Bass.

50. Kouzes, J. M., & Posner, B. Z., 18.

51. Hentschke, G., & Caldwell, B. J.

52. Meier, D. (2012b, September 13).

53. Vitagliano, R., Borasi, R., Jefferson, F., Che, J., & Miller, D. (2008). *Entrepreneurial leadership: Comparing the practices of an entrepreneurial principal and an education entrepreneur*. Paper presented at the annual meeting of the American Educational Research Association, New York City.

54. Macko, A., & Tyszka, T. (2009). Entrepreneurship and risk taking. *Applied Psychology: An International Review, 58*(3), 469–487.

55. Macko, A., & Tyszka, T.

56. Austin, J., Stevenson, H., & Wei-Skillern, J. (2011). Social and commercial entrepreneurship: Same, different, or both? *Revista de Administração, 47*(3), 370–384. doi: http://dx.doi.org/10.1590/S0080-21072012000300003.

57. Browning, Robert: "Ah, but a man's reach should exceed his grasp, Or what's a heaven for?" *Andrea del Sarto*, line 98.

58. TEDxRochester (Producer). (2010, November 1). Warner School of Education–University of Rochester. [videoclip]. Retrieved from http://www.facebook.com/warner.school/posts/178926722161230.

59. Buckingham, M., & Coffman, C. (1999). *First, break all the rules: What the world's greatest managers do differently*. New York City: Simon & Schuster.

60. Borasi, R., & Ames, M.

61. Bornstein, D. (2004). *How to change the world: Social entrepreneurs and the power of new ideas* (p. 3). New York: Oxford University Press.

62. Sergiovanni, T. J. (1998). Leadership as pedagogy, capital development and school effectiveness. *International Journal of Leadership in Education, 1*(1), 37.

63. Steinberg, L., Brown, B. B., & Dornbusch, S. M. (1996). *Beyond the classroom: Why school reform has failed and what parents need to do*. New York: Simon and Schuster.

64. Hamel, G., & LaBarre, P. (2012, October 17). Help us innovate the innovation process, para. 1. Retrieved from http://blogs.hbr.org/cs/2012/10/how_can_we_innovate_the_innova.html.

65. Heifetz, R. A., & Laurie, D. L. (1997). The work of leadership. *Harvard Business Review, 75*(1), 124–134.

66. Jannot, M.

67. Lavaroni, C. W., & Leisey, D. E. (2010). The edupreneur: Bringing the excitement of entrepreneurism to the public schools, para. 10. Retrieved May 8, 2010, from http://www.edentrepreneurs.org/edupreneur.php.

68. Balliro, Beth. Personal communication.

69. Barth, R. (2001). *Learning by heart*. San Francisco: Jossey-Bass, 188.

70. Inspiring innovation. (2002). *Harvard Business Review, 80*(8), 49.

71. Platt, A. D., Tripp, C. E., Ogden, W. R., & Fraser, R. G. (2000). *The skillful leader: Confronting mediocre teaching*. Acton, MA: Ready About Press.

# 2

# MAXIMIZING ENTREPRENEURIAL LEADERSHIP

The desire for innovation in education is incendiary. Entrepreneurial leadership provides the inflammatory spark. Despite all the reservations about motives and risk, there is a constant call for more entrepreneurial leaders in education. This chapter, however, moves away from the fireworks associated with entrepreneurism to consider more carefully this kind of leadership. For some, this chapter will be a detour on the way to more information on how to build entrepreneurial schools. There are strong reasons, however, to take this side trip and try to pin down the meaning of entrepreneurial leadership more carefully.

The concept of entrepreneurial leadership in K–12 schooling suffers on several fronts. First, there are multiple definitions for the entrepreneur in the business world. [1] Despite feverish attention to the topic, there is still significant disagreement about what exactly an entrepreneur is. This was hinted at in chapter 1 and will be illuminated here. One of the purposes of this book is to introduce entrepreneurial leadership, for education in a more sober, rational manner and to offer it as a suitable topic for research and professional development.

Another problem is that the trait approach to entrepreneurialism, which was introduced in the last chapter, is noticeably based on anecdotal evidence and tends to heroic notions of leadership. Reasonable questions have been asked about the reality of these larger-than-life portrayals, and these questions seem even more reasonable in the sedate world of public education. Perhaps, on most days, the elementary school principal featured in chapter 1 was just another plodding bureaucrat. [2]

Related to the heroic tendencies of the stories of entrepreneurial leadership is the distinctly sexist nature of the literature. The preponderance of writing on entrepreneurship features male examples and is written by male scholars, leaving many to wonder how female entrepreneurs might differ. For this reason, the anecdotes in the book have been carefully selected to provide a more balanced view.

Furthermore, most ideas about entrepreneurship in education come from the business world, which is different from public education in some important ways. There is no certainty that educational entrepreneurs, such as Ralph Spezio and Lynn Gatto, who work inside public schools and were featured in chapter 1, share the same traits and behaviors as business entrepreneurs.

This chapter addresses these concerns and takes a closer look at entrepreneurial leadership. The chapter begins with a walk back through economic history, learning from business models of entrepreneurship and thinking about how this might apply to leadership for K–12 schooling. Chapter 1 suggested that entrepreneurial leadership is really a spectrum of behaviors, and that idea is expanded here. This is also a good place to compare entrepreneurial leadership to other leadership styles, such as charismatic, transformational, democratic, or distributed, which will help the reader better appreciate the promise and pitfalls of entrepreneurialism. This chapter concludes with a story about some leaders in a public high school–community college partnership which suggests that entrepreneurial leadership can be enhanced.

## DEFINING ECONOMIC ENTREPRENEURSHIP

An understanding of entrepreneurship comes from the business literature where there are numerous theories on the topic. The word *entrepreneur* is of French origin, meaning "one who undertakes."[3] Richard Cantillon and Jean Baptiste-Say popularized the economic use of the word in the eighteenth century, with the latter describing the entrepreneur as someone who creates value by shifting economic resources "out of an area of lower and into an area of higher productivity and greater yield."[4]

In the twentieth century, the concept of entrepreneurship took on multiple shades of meaning. First, there was Joseph Schumpeter, an Austrian American economist who taught in Europe and at Harvard University and wrote extensively on capitalism and innovation. Schumpeter's idea of entrepreneurship began with a dramatically new innovation, which consisted of something qualitatively new and non-incremental,[5] rather than incremental tweaks on existing technologies. Invariably, the innovation arose in new enterprises. As he wrote,

> Development . . . is then defined by the carrying out of new combinations. . . . New combinations are, as a rule, embodied . . . in firms which generally do not arise out of the old ones but start producing beside them. . . . It is not the owner of a stage coach who builds railways.[6]

The innovation brought a competitive advantage and was often catalytic, stimulating exploitation by other opportunistic entrepreneurs. The wave of innovation disrupted well-established patterns and became a "perennial gale of creative destruction."[7] Entrepreneurial leaders in this mold are inventive, and their comfort with disruptive technologies signals a high risk-tolerance.

Many entrepreneurs, however, are less tolerant of risk.[8] Research in the 1970s led to new conceptions of the entrepreneur through the work of Peter Drucker, Israel Kirzner, and others. Kirzner recognized that many entrepreneurs were more opportunistic than inventive.[9] They were keenly alert to promising opportunities where they could use existing strategies to gain a competitive advantage. There is no new invention, just a deft application of current technologies to gain an advantage. They focus on efficiency rather than originality. This kind of entrepreneur might capitalize on organizational slack internally or market gaps externally to make a financial gain where others have failed to act.

Schumpeter and Kirzner offer contrasting views of entrepreneurship. Schumpeter described an iconoclastic figure. In contrast, the Kirznerian entrepreneur was a "coordinator and facilitator" who brought ideas, resources, and people together.[10] Schumpeter's entrepreneur was the breakthrough innovator, while Kirzner's was the early exploiter.[11] Where Schumpeter highlighted the first game-changing innovation, Kirzner and others focused on the many other entrepreneurs who sprang on the opportunity and fed the chain reaction of "creative destruction." Whereas Schumpeter described the innovator-entrepreneur, Kirzner depicted the producer-entrepreneur.[12] Schumpeter described opportunity creation, while Kirzner emphasized opportunity discovery. For Schumpeter, the primary characteristics were ingenuity and creativity,[13] while for Kirzner alertness was the defining characteristic. For Schumpeter, the entrepreneur was an agent of change; for Kirzner, he was an exploiter of change.

## THE SOCIAL ENTREPRENEUR

The interest in entrepreneurial leadership, the premise for this book, has spawned a host of related terms—social entrepreneur, edupreneur, policy entrepreneur, intrapreneur, and others—each of which offers a new angle on the concept. The term *social entrepreneur* was first coined by Bill Drayton, who founded an organization devoted to investing in social enterprises. Drayton wrote,

> Whenever society is stuck or has an opportunity to seize a new opportunity, it needs an entrepreneur to see the opportunity and then to turn that vision into a realistic idea and then a reality and then, indeed, the new pattern all across society. We need such entrepreneurial leadership at least as much in education and human rights as we do in communications and hotels. This is the work of social entrepreneurs. [14]

Just as the concept of economic entrepreneurship still suffers from multiple meanings after a century of research, the idea of social entrepreneurship is not well established either and relies heavily on anecdotal rather than empirical evidence. One review identified thirty-seven different definitions of social entrepreneurship in the literature from 1991 to 2009. [15] As a result, research in this field is still emerging. [16]

A commonly cited example of a social entrepreneur, who is widely known and respected, is Mohammed Yunus, who pioneered the concept of micro-loans to help indigenous Bengalis gain financial security. [17] As a social entrepreneur, Yunus founded a bank that provided very small loans—in the range of twenty-five dollars—to poor people who could not qualify for a traditional bank loan. Most of his borrowers were women who went on to become profit-making entrepreneurs, thus gaining financial security. Saint Francis of Assisi and Florence Nightingale were social entrepreneurs, but most examples tend to be largely unknown. In his book on this topic, David Bornstein listed thirty-four world-shaking social entrepreneurs, including Mohammed Yunus; what is most startling is that most of the names are obscure. [18]

Social entrepreneurs have different priorities; they try to maximize social capital rather than financial capital. [19] *Social capital* is a term that places a value on one's relational or communal assets. The term is increasingly used in education to help explain the achievement gap. Many urban students, for example, lack the social networks that would open the doors to jobs, a college education, and advancement. All of the educational entrepreneurs described in chapter 1 are social entrepreneurs.

On the surface, social entrepreneurs are motivated by the social good whereas business entrepreneurs are motivated by making money. However, this distinction is shortsighted. The research demonstrates that economic gain is not always the primary motive for business entrepreneurs. Schumpeter argued that entrepreneurs are often motivated by "the desire to found a private dynasty, or the will to conquer in competitive battle, or the sheer joy of creation."[20] Other motivations will be explored in this chapter.

To complicate things, business profits can have significant social value in terms of providing jobs, lifting income, offering better products, and improving lifestyle choices. Some businesses pride themselves on their social values, such as improving the environment or bettering health care. Business is not just about making money.

At the same time, many social entrepreneurs engage in profit-making ventures as a way to expand their operations.[21] Lynn Gatto, who invented the state-shaped cookie cutters for her students and helped create a new science curriculum, marketed her inventions and was able to raise funds for additional classroom projects. However, one can see that her primary motive was to benefit her students. Deborah Meier has very successfully marketed her writings and is a popular and well-paid speaker. In this way, she helped launch the small schools movement in America, even as she was able to provide for herself, her family, and those first urban schools. However, the pursuit of social, rather than economic, value is clearly a dominating motive.

Economic enterprise is often defined as three sectors, where the first is private enterprise, the second is public service, and the third is non-profit work. Business entrepreneurship is in the private (first) sector and social entrepreneurship in the non-profit sector of society. In this way, many philanthropic organizations are also considered examples of social entrepreneurship. However, some first-sector enterprises can be socially motivated. Furthermore, a lot of public, second-sector work, where compensation often lags behind top positions in the first sector, is socially motivated. Obviously, the entrepreneurial leaders described in this book were working in the public sector (K–12 education), rather than the non-profit sector, but they were social entrepreneurs just the same.[22] Therefore, some define social entrepreneurship as spanning all three sectors.[23] This is particularly true in resource procurement; social entrepreneurs are likely to go wherever necessary to find the support and resources they need to fulfill their vision.

Social entrepreneurs are not sector-bound.[24] Like most entrepreneurs, social entrepreneurs think outside the box of traditional answers and approaches. They do more than just think outside, however; they want to ignore the boundaries that separate the non-profit, government, and business sectors. Their boundary-spanning approach applies to the process of scavenging resources; they succeed, in part, by mobilizing resources from these noncontiguous domains in new ways to create social value.[25] Spezio, for example, tapped the business community and the non-profit sector to marshal the resources he needed for his students.

David Hodgson, who is the founder of another organization that provides seed money to aspiring social entrepreneurs, says they are "holistic thinkers" who "believe in an integrated approach."[26] Their thinking often moves beyond traditional private, public, and non-profit sector models and imagines a fourth sector that combines resources from all multiple sectors. The second half of this book will explore more deeply the strategies of social entrepreneurs.

The boundary-spanning nature of social entrepreneurs can be seen in their value creation as well. Business and social entrepreneurs both create value, but social entrepreneurs are less likely to struggle with ownership. Business entrepreneurs must create market value or they will not remain in business. Dees points out, however, that "markets do not work as well for social entrepreneurs."[27] Their products are harder to evaluate financially and are often provided to people who cannot afford to pay. This is one of the main limitations with applying a business model to socially conscious work.

Business entrepreneurs must think competitively to survive in the market. They are more likely to guard their innovations rather than share them freely. Social entrepreneurs do the opposite. Independent of market valuations, they are more likely to share resources and ideas to increase social value. They work cooperatively instead of competitively. Free from addressing the bottom line for their investors, they are more likely to seek the public good instead of the private good.

In conclusion, many scholars emphasize the *motive* (where the primary motive of the social entrepreneur is social value creation) and the *mission* (being the identification and solution of an insufferable social problem) when they want to distinguish the social entrepreneur from the economic entrepreneur, while acknowledging that the character traits are largely the same.[28]

Other new, socially motivated movements, such as sustainable entrepreneurship, community-based entrepreneurship, and indigenous entrepreneurship, confuse the definition.[29] Other scholars try to separate out social service activities from social activism, arguing that too broad a conceptualization of social entrepreneurship leaves the field vulnerable to criticism.[30] Some of these alternatives may simply be variations on the size of socially entrepreneurial enterprises.

Indeed, some researchers describe a hierarchy of social entrepreneurship.[31] The social *bricoleur* acts locally, combining people and resources in a network to address needs in his/her own backyard.[32] Ralph Spezio, an elementary school principal in Rochester, New York, is a good example. These kinds of social service activities are sometimes excluded from the definition of social entrepreneurship since they may not be self-sustaining or replicable.[33] However, they meet the definition of *motive, mission,* and *character* suggested earlier, and because of their localness, they offer tailor-made solutions to tough problems.

On a larger scale, the *social constructivist* builds systems to address the needs of adults, often filling gaps left by a welfare state.[34] The innovations of the social constructivist are scalable, meaning they can be replicated and disseminated for greater impact. After years of working to raise student achievement, Ralph Spezio discovered that many of his elementary school children had dangerously high blood levels of lead, which is a neurological toxin. He began a campaign to alert the public to the dangers of lead paint, which spread beyond his own school to the district and, eventually, to the national stage.[35] In this case, Spezio was a social constructivist. A second example is Ted Sizer, the founder of the Coalition of Essential Schools, which has been slowly scaled up to a nationwide network of over eight hundred schools. Sometimes, this is termed *institutional* entrepreneurship, where a new kind of institution is created with new cultural norms, standards, and structures.[36] Many social activists operate at this level as they seek to change institutional culture.

Finally, the *social engineer* creates entire social systems, which span multiple institutions and can more effectively address large-scale social needs.[37] These innovations often have a revolutionary effect. Bill Drayton had this in mind when he wrote,

> Social entrepreneurs have the same core temperament as their industry-creating, business entrepreneur peers but instead use their talents to solve social problems on a society-wide scale. . . . Both types of entrepreneur recognize when a part of society is stuck and provide new ways to get it unstuck. Each type of entrepreneur envisages a systemic change, identifies the jujitsu points that will allow him or her to tip the whole society onto this new path, and then persists and persists until the job is done.[38]

Horace Mann, considered the father of the common school movement in America, was an early social engineer. Inevitably, social engineers are both lauded and loathed because of the size and impact of their work.

To summarize, entrepreneurial leadership, whether in business or education, is not defined as one thing but rather conceptualized along a series of gradients, which can be used to understand the dynamic nature of the concept. First, entrepreneurs develop innovations, which is another term that presents a range of meaning. Chapter 1 described how the word *innovation* can mean *the thing* itself or the *process* of innovating all the way to commercial *implementation* of the original idea. This chapter introduced entrepreneurial leadership with a second gradient stretching from Schumpeter's disruptive innovativeness to Kirzner's opportunistic exploitation. Possibly, these gradients overlap; Schumpeter's attention was on the innovation itself and the ensuing disruptive process, while Kirzner was more interested in how the process presented opportunities for commercialization.

There is a third gradient in this definition, which stretches from economic to social entrepreneurship, where one end is driven purely by profits and the other by a view of the public good. Entrepreneurial leadership can also be conceptualized among the private, public, and non-profit sectors, with a recognition that some social entrepreneurs may operate in all three sectors. And finally, educational entrepreneurs can be classified as *bricoleurs*, *social constructivists*, or, on the largest scale, *social engineers*. These gradients reflect the diversity of the field but enable more careful definition.

There is no end to the many terms created to capture some aspect of the entrepreneurial leader. There is the *policy entrepreneur*, an "idea champion" who specializes in big ideas for educational reform,[39] the *public sector entrepreneur*,[40] and the *edupreneur* (who works exclusively within K–12 schooling).[41] The multiplication of terms becomes disorienting after a while, which is why they are not used in this book.

There is one more notable term, which is important for this discussion. Most entrepreneurial work is not done by the person at the top of the organization. In 1985 Pinchot first described the *intrapreneur*, who was an entrepreneurially minded individual working within the ranks of a large organization.[42] Often, these employees invent something and then leave the corporation to pursue their creative dream, which might result in a new business, even a competitor. Many big businesses began looking for ways to retain the innovative spirit internally.

This is a sixth spectrum for understanding entrepreneurship in education. At one end is the independent entrepreneur; at the other end is the intrapreneur who is buried within a larger organization. While entrepreneurs innovate for themselves, intrapreneurs innovate for the organization in which they work.[43] For obvious reasons, intrapreneurs depend on someone in the organization to recognize their work. The public school entrepreneurs described in this book all worked near the dependent end.

There are many entrepreneurial leaders in education who work outside the realm of K–12 schooling to offer innovative services and reformative ideas.[44] Many of them enjoy the relative independence found at the other end of this spectrum. There are many examples, including the founders of Teach for America, New Leaders for New Schools, the National Institute for School Leadership, and others. They share many of the traits and behaviors described in chapter 1, and they could be positioned on the gradients presented earlier in this chapter. This book, however, is written to draw attention to the educational *intrapreneurs* who still work within K–12 schooling and to offer them some recognition and encouragement.

This chapter began with a short critique of the progress on defining entrepreneurial leadership, including the androcentric nature of the research.[45] Even Bornstein's book, which deliberately showcased female as well as male social entrepreneurs, included only ten female examples out of a total list of thirty-four notables' names.[46] Gender is increasingly considered in studying business entrepreneurship, but less so with research on social entrepreneurship. This is unfortunate, since this is one area where the female perspective might shine through, since women have greater representation in the non-profit sector than in the private and public sectors.[47] This sector better addresses their natural concerns for children, health, education, and family, for example. Nevertheless, men still disproportionately run third-sector organizations while women occupy lower positions and are paid less money for the same work.[48] This is similar to the state of affairs in public education. All this implies that more study is needed, using non-androcentric lenses, to better understand gender differences in social entrepreneurship.

## ENTREPRENEURIAL LEADERSHIP VERSUS OTHER LEADERSHIP THEORIES

The first chapter first looked at entrepreneurial leadership in terms of character *traits*, such as individualism and risk-tolerance, and then in terms of leadership *behaviors*, such as communicating a vision or leveraging resources. Researchers have also described certain leadership *styles*, where each style is a distinct set of leadership behaviors, such as *democratic, charismatic*, or *transformational*. There is not a definitive list. Comparisons can help clarify the strengths and drawbacks of an entrepreneurial leadership style. For example, entrepreneurial leaders are often charismatic, especially when they are talking about their idea, but there are important differences.

In recent years, researchers have demonstrated that the best leaders may actually have more than one leadership style, where the expressed style would be contingent on the nature of the challenge presented to the organization and the nature of the leader's team. This is situational leadership. For example, Daniel Goleman wrote an important article in the Harvard Business Review in 2000, which identified six leadership styles: commanding, visionary, affiliative, democratic, pacesetting, and coaching.[49] Each style was based upon certain emotional intelligence capabilities, which was the main focus of Goleman's research, such as self-awareness, self-management, social awareness, and social skill. The leadership styles were suitable for various organizational challenges, which might include team-building, professional development, increasing overall motivation, or turning around a company. All this makes for a nice chart of situations and leadership styles. Goleman was particularly interested in how each style affected the organizational climate, which ultimately impacts financial outcomes. His point was that "leaders with the best results do not rely on only one leadership style; they use most of them in a given week—seamlessly and in different measure—depending on the business situation."[50]

For Goleman, the most effective leaders judge the situation—the workers and the problem—and adjust their style to achieve their goals. Entrepreneurial leaders, however, are different. Their leadership is not primarily characterized by their ability to get along with people, but by their ability to find a new approach. They think less about the situation at hand and more about other outside-the-box alternatives. Faced with a challenge, one of Goleman's leaders would ask what *internal* adjustment in personal style must be made to most efficiently meet the challenge with the available workers. An entrepreneurial leader might ask what *external* approach—redefining the problem or finding a new solution—could help move everything forward.

Entrepreneurial leaders vary in the degree to which they possess Goleman's emotional intelligence capabilities. One should assume that some are visionary, some are commanding, some are affiliative, and so on. In truth, some entrepreneurial leaders are not good climate-builders. What they have in common, however—the thing that binds them together as a group—is the new idea. They might dig deeper and find the true source of the problem. They might find a better solution outside the company. They might decide to outsource the problem and avoid the company employees altogether.

Where Goleman's leadership styles are ranked according to goal accomplishment, entrepreneurial leadership is equally consumed with goal identification. However, entrepreneurial leaders are more likely to discover new routes to the goal and less likely to change their leadership style. Two scholars who study entrepreneurial leadership explained that leaders in general tend toward "simplifying reality" and "clarifying causality and strengthening control over it," whereas entrepreneurial leaders tend toward "generating new realities."[51] Goleman's leaders work to regain control; entrepreneurial leaders are more likely to relinquish control, even to invite chaos, in the process of seeking alternative solutions.

Entrepreneurial leaders are solution-oriented, not people-oriented, by definition. Once they have a solution, they might very well employ one or more of Goleman's leadership styles, based on their emotional intelligence. Presumably, this is one reason why some entrepreneurs are more successful than others.

Entrepreneurial leaders may lack emotional intelligence capabilities. There is little research on this topic. However, research on social entrepreneurialism has identified four possible drawbacks for this leadership style. First, because these leaders are selective about co-workers, they can be perceived as exclusionary. Since they are often driven by ambition, they can make excessive demands on team members and can even restrict personal freedoms.[52] Entrepreneurial leaders are sometimes inclined to make quick decisions to avoid missing a window of opportunity.[53] Once they are consumed by a vision, they are less likely to listen to reason or to pay attention to obstacles. These tendencies are not universal, of course, but they underscore the reality that every leadership style carries both strengths and liabilities.

## MORE LEADERSHIP STYLES

The transformational leadership style has been popular since the 1990s but was first postulated by Burns.[54] He first described the transactional leadership style, which is a bargaining approach akin to "you scratch my back and I'll scratch yours." Transactional leaders may lack charisma but derive their authority from formal contracts and informal agreements. Consequently, the followers are unlikely to volunteer more than is required. In contrast, transformational leaders "form a relationship of mutual stimulation and elevation that converts followers into leaders and may convert leaders into moral agents."[55] Their leadership often inspires followers to go above and beyond their work contract. Later formulations of the theory described the "four I's" of transformational leadership, which include individual consideration for followers, intellectual stimulation by helping followers see problems in new ways, inspirational motivation in mission and vision, and idealized influence through personal modeling.[56]

Chapter 1 reported that entrepreneurial leaders see problems in new ways, often provide visionary leadership, and model the process through their hands-on approach. For this reason, one might expect to find a correlation between transformational leadership and the entrepreneurial leadership style. Two scholars looked at leadership in 140 elementary schools in Israel and found that transformational leadership most closely associated with Kirzner's opportunistic entrepreneurism, rather than the more inventive and disruptive form.[57] These leaders were better at recognizing and test-driving good ideas than at creating brand-new ideas, which is not surprising in the conservative environment of public education. Comparing other leadership styles, the scholars reported, "Transformational leadership sets the most favorable managerial circumstances for organizational entrepreneurial activism."[58]

Transformational leaders are famous for their relationships. They don't so much transform the structures or core technology as they do the followers. They transform people, who in turn improve company outcomes. Entrepreneurial leaders are not famous for their relationships, for that is not the focus of their leadership. Each leadership style offers a different emphasis, and they certainly overlap. Transformational leadership in education produces a positive working climate and may or may not lead to innovations; entrepreneurial leadership is defined by those innovations.

Recent scholarship focuses on distributive leadership, which is not so much a leadership style as a leadership phenomenon.[59] Under close scrutiny, one discovers that the activities and tasks of leadership are not confined to one person, but are shared by multiple people working in a situation on a particular problem, which includes inherent social structures and language. The leaders affect one another and are, in turn, affected by the environment, even as they affect the same. The leadership phenomenon is *distributed among* the individuals and the situation. As a result, the organizational leader is influenced by the followers and the environment; the ultimate leadership is the collaborative outcome of this unit.

Entrepreneurial leadership is different in that these leaders are not confined to the context at hand. They will simply look for another context, meaning new partners or another environment, rather than abandon their idea. These leaders might turn to different coworkers or another department. The business world is full of examples of creative

leaders who walked away from a corporation entirely to pursue an entrepreneurial innovation. The entrepreneurial leader would not deny
the reality of a distributed leadership but might be more selective in
choosing the team with which leadership is distributed because the
innovative idea is paramount.

Finally, chapter 1 presented the difference between technical and
adaptive challenges in schools and other organizations. Adaptive challenges imply that one doesn't know what needs to be done in the face of
a problem. There is no obvious solution at hand. People have to discover and learn new approaches, new attitudes, and new habits. In this
sense, entrepreneurial leadership is all about adaptive problems, not
technical ones. If the solution already lies within the organization, then
there is no innovation and, by definition, no entrepreneurial leadership.[60]

Heifetz and his colleagues were less interested in particular leadership styles but more concerned about organizational learning. If the
leader tried to offer technical "fixes," then the organization would not
learn and grow and, inevitably, the problem would resurface. When the
problem was technical, the leader could delegate the work or do it
himself; but when the problem was adaptive, *the people with the problem had to do the work*. Chapter 1 established that entrepreneurial
leadership is nice for adaptive learning, but this chapter offers an important distinction.

Here is a simple illustration of a technical versus an adaptive solution:

> When your car breaks down, you go to a mechanic. Most of the time,
> the mechanic can fix it. However, if the car breaks down because of
> the way members of the family use it, the problem will probably
> happen again. The mechanic might be able to get the car on the road
> once more. But by continuing to deal with it as a purely technical
> problem a mechanic can solve, the family may end up avoiding the
> underlying issues demanding adaptive work, such as how to persuade
> the mother to stop drinking and driving, or the grandfather to give
> up his driver's license, or the teenagers to be more cautious.[61]

This is a great illustration. Novice leaders, determined to be problem-
solvers, keep taking the car to the mechanic. Wise leaders use well-
accepted leadership strategies to confront the family about their driving
habits, which is real adaptive work. Admittedly, this can get ugly. What
if the mother has no intention of giving up alcohol or the grandfather
refuses to stop driving? Sometimes, people just refuse to own the problem, so the car keeps getting damaged or the protagonist cuts off family
members.

Entrepreneurial leaders, meanwhile, are off thinking in new directions. What if cars could be made that would not break down? Would it be possible to invent a car that a drunk could not start? What if society had a blanket policy to test the driving ability of all elderly drivers so this grandfather does not feel singled out? What kind of drivers' education class would make teenagers even *more* cautious than adults? What if we had a *better way* to build collective ownership and responsibility within the family?

Entrepreneurial leaders own the problem because they like problems, so they are less likely to give it away. Rather than seeing the problem as a threat, this kind of leader senses opportunity for a new approach, a new solution, a captivating idea. As Michael Fullan said, "Problems are our friends."[62] This is not naïve leadership, but just a different way of looking at things. Entrepreneurial leaders like to think about the problem; they brainstorm (if they are inventive) or they keep their eyes and ears open (if they are opportunistic), but they are always looking for a better way to do things.

In their leadership book, Heifetz and Linsky wrote a chapter called "Give the Work Back." They wrote, "Solutions are achieved when 'the people with the problem' go through a process together to become 'the people with the solution.' The issues have to be internalized, owned, and ultimately resolved by the relevant parties to achieve enduring success."[63] Entrepreneurial leaders are often looking for a more efficient way to achieve the same goal, so they look for solutions.

One might expect that there would be less organizational learning under entrepreneurial leaders. Having a promising idea is not enough. Michael Fullan, who has written so prolifically and powerfully on educational reform, stated that, "it is not enough to have the best ideas."[64] Implementation, experimentation, and, ultimately, institutionalization are required. This is the *commercial* end of entrepreneurial leadership, and, admittedly, some leaders are better at this than others.

This is where other leadership styles can make a world of difference. The entrepreneurial leader with a good solution, who is also transformational, is more likely to achieve collective ownership and implementation than the same leader with a transactional leadership style. This can be more or less important, depending on the size of the innovative solution.

> Leadership supporting an innovation must be consistent with the order of magnitude of the change represented by that innovation. If leadership techniques do not match the order of change required by an innovation, the innovation will probably fail regardless of its merits.[65]

Earlier, this chapter described three kinds of social entrepreneurs: the social *bricoleur*, the social constructivist, and the social engineer. Obviously, the social engineer would require a more sophisticated repertoire of leadership strategies to achieve success than the social *bricoleur*. Entrepreneurial leaders can also expand their repertoire of leadership styles and become more effective on the spectrum of inventing and implementing new ideas.

Entrepreneurial leaders are not detrimental to organizational learning. Many organizations, both in K–12 schooling and outside education, struggle to be more entrepreneurial. The entrepreneur within their ranks provokes adaptive change. Creating an innovative culture is an adaptive challenge in itself. Indeed, many consider entrepreneurship to be more of an organizational phenomenon than an individual one. This is the focus of chapter 3.

## MAXIMIZING ENTREPRENEURISM

While research on entrepreneurism in the business world is rife, the scholarship on this kind of leadership in K–12 schooling is remarkably scarce. Little is known about whether a school leader can learn to lead more entrepreneurially. In addition, no one knows whether an opportunistic kind of entrepreneur can develop into a more original, inventive entrepreneur.

Israeli scholar Ori Eyal developed the Public School Entrepreneurial Inventory (PSEI) in order to measure entrepreneurialism inside K–12 schools through the eyes of teachers.[66] The PSEI measures two variables commonly associated with corporate entrepreneurialism: leader proactivity and organizational innovativeness. Proactivity was defined as "the principal's willingness to initiate actions within the school . . . not imposed by higher authorities."[67] Innovativeness was defined as the "quantity of innovations implemented in an organization . . . in a given time period and their impact (first- or second-degree change) on the organization."[68] In this way, the survey collected data on both principal and organizational characteristics. Other corporate characteristics, such as risk-taking, were not measured because the relationship to entrepreneurial activity was not linear.[69]

Working from these two variables, the researchers identified four leadership styles, which are listed here and visually represented in figure 2.1:

- *Conservative* leaders emphasized "stability, continuity, and maintenance of the status quo."[70]
- *Calculating* leaders were "reactive in nature," relying on "historical improvements approved by the system" and applying them in step-by-step fashion.[71] This kind of leadership tends to incremental and predictable change.
- Initiating leaders showed *opportunistic entrepreneurialism* with a "flurry strategy" of borrowing and testing many ideas in a "trial and error culture" while making few permanent adoptions.[72] This leadership is opportunistic and Kirznerian.
- Finally, vigorous leaders demonstrated *radical entrepreneurialism*, featuring "discontinuous, frame-breaking changes," while discarding "conventional operating practices."[73] The description is very Schumpeterian.

Eyal and his colleagues were curious about the prevalence of these leadership styles. They surveyed ten teachers from each of 140 Israeli elementary schools, using the PSEI, in order to explore the relative distribution of entrepreneurial characteristics among school leaders. The teachers perceived 5 percent of their principals as conservative, 38.7 percent as calculating, 45.4 percent as initiating, and a mere 10.9 percent as vigorous, frame-breaking leaders.[74] The last group had a leadership style which was a "dramatic departure from current organizational strategy, independent of authorities in the system." These leaders were able "to go against the current organizational structure,

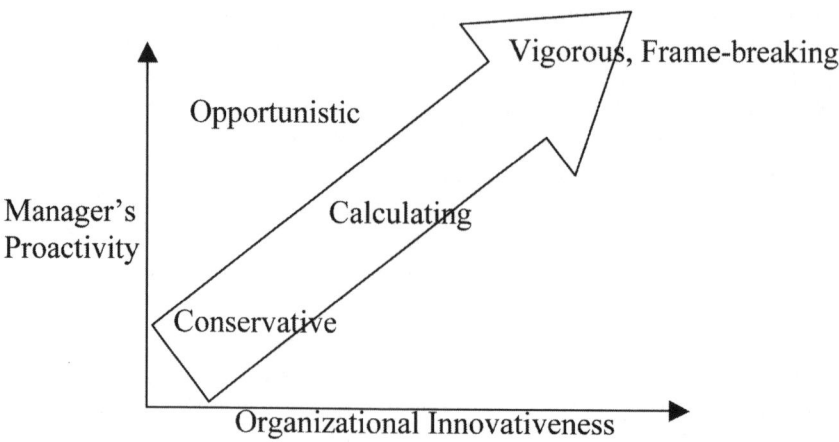

**Figure 2.1.   Theoretical Entrepreneurial Strategies**

operating as if it did not exist."[75] They were "free of existing constraints of the environment."[76]

While not perfect, the survey of teachers provided an instructive array of entrepreneurial leadership, which raises new questions. Can entrepreneurial leadership be increased? Can calculating or opportunistic leadership be turned into vigorous, frame-breaking entrepreneurial leadership?

## A CASE STUDY: THE EARLY COLLEGE PROGRAM

In 2007 a high school guidance counselor in a small, very typical suburban town in the northeast corner of the United States was worried about the college readiness of her students, where the top 25 percent sailed through high school and college, but the long-term success of the majority of students was doubtful. She had just read an article about early college high schools, a comparatively new phenomenon in America where school-university partnerships allow students to take college coursework as early as ninth grade. Since her high school already had a partnership with a nearby community college, she contacted one of the college deans and shared the article, wondering if they could start an early college high school. Soon, they invited others to join the brainstorming, including the principal, and passed around more articles.

What makes this case interesting is that the dean and the principal were both accomplished entrepreneurs. The dean had worked in the business sector and started a number of small companies, while the principal was both the son of a business entrepreneur and owner of a chocolate business, which he ran out of his garage with his wife. The guidance counselor, who borrowed the original idea from the literature, was also an outside-the-box thinker. Like many entrepreneurs, they shared some bravado and a "damn-the-torpedoes" approach that helped them plow forward with the idea. At one point, the principal shared their idea with the state commissioner of education, who declined financial support. The principal was unfazed; as he told the state leader, "We're going to do this with you or without you!"

Meeting for two years with other college leaders, the district superintendent, and selected teachers, this team took an idea borrowed from the literature and turned it into a college readiness program tailor-made for their school. They invited the author of this book to join the team as a research/evaluator, and they crafted the following goals:

- More students would earn college credit before high school graduation.
- More students would take Advanced Placement courses in their junior and senior years.
- More students would attend college within three months of high school graduation.
- Fewer students would need remedial coursework when they attended college.
- More students would complete a college certificate or degree within four years of graduating from high school.

Arguing that the top quartile students were already in line to meet these goals, the planning team decided to target the two middle academic quartiles of students, beginning in grade ten. The final early college program was unique in several particulars. The college courses were offered during the regular school day, rather than after school or during the summer. They were offered at the high school, not on the college campus. In this way, students were able to fully participate in other high school activities, such as sports, arts programs, and clubs; their high school experience was not curtailed, and they were not cut off from other friends (this has been a complaint of some other early college high school students). At the same time, they were a visible model for the entire high school.

The college courses, which began in tenth grade, offered concurrent credit, meaning students could earn credits on both their high school and college transcripts while participating. The college courses were not layered on top of a full high school schedule but substituted for part of the high school curriculum. Their college transcript was indistinguishable from the adult model, so the credits these students were earning could never be rejected. In truth, the high school students were fully enrolled as regular college students with identification cards, email addresses, and access to the library, campus tutoring services, and online academic learning platforms.

The support structures offered to these students were intensive so the success rate was very high.[77] Students in the tenth grade, for example, took three college courses that were fully integrated in a learning community model. The learning community model, where new students move as a cohort through a set of integrated courses, is a common approach on community college campuses.[78] American literature was combined with a course in US history, so students read original texts in their historical contexts and wrote one set of analytical papers. The courses were team-taught, which decreased the student/teacher ratio. In addition, a third course on college success strategies, normally required of all incoming freshmen college students, was integrated with the literature and history program. In tenth grade, students were given more than twice the time to complete college course requirements, which boosted the success rate. As they proceeded through higher grades, the time was reduced and supports were removed so that by the last half of their senior year, they were taking regular courses on the college campus, sitting alongside regular adult students.

Finding permanent financial support for early college high school programs is a predictable and significant challenge.[79] The planning team wrestled with this dilemma for a long time. As with most entrepreneurs, they did not want to be hampered by unreliable state grants or outside funding, so they created a model of shared financial responsibility. Parents paid a flat fee each year, which was less than half the normal tuition, so they saved money on the cost of college. The college reduced its tuition by 35 percent, and the district picked up the remaining costs, which varied depending on the number of students enrolled. A local foundation agreed to assist a few struggling families. With this plan, the early college program could proceed regardless of the vagaries of state support.[80]

In the first year of the early college program, each of the thirty-one students earned nine college credits. By graduation, twenty-six students had earned twelve or more credits and twenty-two students had accumulated twenty credits or more. The highest-earning student completed thirty-four college credits. With more than one year of college completed, at substantial savings, these students were well on their way to full-time attendance and graduation from a two- or four-year college experience.

We know that students with earned college credits on their transcript are more likely to enroll in college right after graduation.[81] Furthermore, these students gain academic momentum and are more likely to persist in college. One national leader on the issue of college readiness was very specific on the benefit of accumulated credits: "Six is good, nine is better, and twelve is a guarantee of momentum."[82]

This case study high school succeeded in multiplying the pathways to college. First, there was the traditional route, already embraced by the top 25 percent of students, which led through honors courses, Advanced Placement, and dual enrollment courses to college. This pathway was supplemented with the early college program, which invited academically average students, not on the honors track, to also get ready for college. In this way, the high school greatly increased the number of students who were ready for college.[83]

The three entrepreneurs began to share their story in regional gatherings of guidance counselors, secondary school administrators, and higher education leaders. They also presented in national conferences. Soon, the early college design began to spread to other high schools in the region. A nearby urban high school duplicated the plan and began to work with the same community college. In another county, a second high school launched a similar program with another community college. A high school in the next state adopted the plan.

While it is exciting to share the successes of this early college program, what is interesting for the purposes of this chapter is to consider the evolution of the entrepreneurial leadership over the four-year course of planning. The top leaders from the college and high school were already entrepreneurial. Using the gradients developed earlier, they were opportunistic, rather than inventive entrepreneurs; they recognized a good idea when they saw it and ran with it. They borrowed the idea of the early college high school and initially planned a program similar to those across the country. However, meeting biweekly for over two years with other administrators, teachers, parents, and even students, they began to tweak every aspect of the program, addressing funding, credit accumulation and transfer, accreditation concerns, student support, team-teaching, guidance counseling, parental engagement, and countless other issues. Over time, a theory of action began to emerge.

- Students came first.
- The target was the academically "middle" students.
- All students must succeed, since failure would only reinforce the perception that some were not cut out for college.
- Students in the early college program would still enjoy a normal high school experience.
- Shared responsibility meant that many hands shared in support for the students.
- "Whatever it takes" meant that leaders would find a way to overcome every obstacle.
- Neither the lack of state funds or grants would keep the project from going forward.
- Evaluate everything.

The planning team was unusual in some ways. Their meetings were regular and well-attended by college and district leaders, but it was the middle managers who fine-tuned the program. They made a concerted effort to engage key stakeholders without giving up control of the emerging project—a very entrepreneurial trait. The agendas were informal, quickly assembled, and open to change. There was no formal memorandum of agreement until the third year, which primarily addressed funding issues. The participants met because they wanted to, not because they were required by a formal agreement, grant requirements, or institutional mandates.

In time, what began as an idea borrowed from the literature—the early college high school idea—evolved into something that was new and unprecedented. More importantly, what began as opportunistic entrepreneurialism evolved into a more advanced, vigorous, framebreaking brand of entrepreneurial leadership. At a time when state- and grant-funded early college high schools were being planted all over the country, this team invented an affordable, self-sustaining, replicable model that was all locally supported.[84] The leaders were able to articulate this plan and share it with other leaders across the state at a time when high schools everywhere were struggling with college readiness and state funding for dual enrollment was unreliable. This was a framebreaking innovation that began to spread to other high schools.

Furthermore, the early college program promoted a new, more ecological model of college readiness. Whereas most scholars focus on the skills of the graduating student, the participants in this study learned that college readiness is a community challenge. The parents had to gain familiarity with a college culture that included academic and financial expectations, registration deadlines, bursars, invoices, tutoring services, and online resources. The high school guidance counselors grew in their understanding of how college transcripts and financial aid are closely linked. Meanwhile, college counselors and faculty members gained a better understanding of how to support new students.[85]

The gradients, which were developed earlier in this chapter, can be used to analyze this case study. Using figure 1, one can see that the entrepreneurial team moved from an opportunistic to a more framebreaking style of leadership. Their work was less Kirznerian and more Schumpeterian in nature. On the whole, they were operating in the public sector as leaders in a public high school and public community college. However, two of the leaders transferred in skills learned in the private, business world. They found they could turn to a local educational foundation to provide small amounts of support to struggling families. Thus they incorporated the third, non-profit sector in their strategy.

In the developmental years, the leaders ran the early college program without reward. The principal, guidance counselor, and college dean donated thousands of hours to the project without regard to compensation. For them, this was part of the job of being a visionary leader. Furthermore, the teachers who volunteered to work in the program donated countless hours to learn new skills in team-teaching, integrating curricula, and supporting students in challenging coursework. They

were all social entrepreneurs pursuing the public good for both struggling students and their cash-strapped parents.

Over time, however, the leaders realized that donating time to a
program that was spreading to other schools was not sustainable. They
developed their early college educational innovation into a non-profit
business. Under the umbrella of the college, they offered the new program as a package for purchase to nearby districts, complete with curriculum, consulting services, and program evaluation. The program was
able to generate funds, which would support expansion across many
districts. In other words, they began to move along the motives spectrum which has altruistic social entrepreneurship at one end and the
pursuit of profits at the other end.

And finally, the entrepreneurial leaders were just *bricoleurs* in the
initial years of the early college program. The dean and the principal
created the early college package, which could be marketed to other
districts. The principal reached retirement age and left the district, but
he continued to work for the college by promoting the model to other
high schools. Because of her ability to overcome obstacles and get
things done, the dean was reassigned by the college to new challenges
that took advantage of her entrepreneurial leadership. A new college
administrator was assigned to the early college programs, which were
now operating in multiple high schools; her goal was to create systems
of communication, publication, evaluation, and financing, which would
allow the early college efforts to expand and grow and differentiate
indefinitely. She was a *social constructivist.* The work evolved and required new degrees of entrepreneurial leadership.

Chapter 1 defined entrepreneurial leadership this way: the entrepreneurial leader begins with a question—*how can we do this better?*—
and then turns the ideas into policies, programs, and enterprises, which
have intellectual, social, and/or economic value. In reality, many entrepreneurs are not able (or interested) in taking an innovation to the next
stage of development, especially if it distracts from the fun creative
work. As a result, some researchers point out the need for a "champion"
who can pick up the innovation ball and run with it.[86] Often, the champion is a *social constructivist* who has the patience to think about the
larger systems needed for development and dissemination. This idea is
developed further in chapter 3.

## CONCLUSION

There have been very few studies of entrepreneurial leadership in the public schools. Using the literature from business and social entrepreneurship, this chapter offered several gradients against which one can gauge and, perhaps, better understand entrepreneurial leadership in education.

For some readers, there will be understandable impatience with this focus on definitions. Entrepreneurs are doers; they don't want to get bogged down with definitions. Scholars, however, know that a good definition is the first step on the road to teaching, measuring, and maximizing entrepreneurial leadership. Clear definitions enable everyone to better spot the entrepreneurs, for encouragement and mutual learning. At the same time, inaccurate conceptualizations of entrepreneurial leadership invite criticism. Sometimes, the term becomes a catch-word for every kind of effective leadership, a concept so broad that it becomes meaningless.

No doubt, this conceptualization is murky. The ambiguity of this book simply reflects the larger field of scholarship on entrepreneurship. Business scholars have offered varying definitions of entrepreneurship for centuries without resolving the issue or coming to agreement. And yet there is intense interest in the topic because no one doubts that the thing—whatever it is—is real. Entrepreneurs start enterprises, whether economic or social, and have a significant impact on the world. They represent the cutting edge of innovation. These individuals are out there; they are invaluable and interesting even though one can't quite put one's finger on them.

Entrepreneurial leadership is a leadership style, which compares and contrasts with other leadership styles, such as the transformational or distributed leadership style. These kinds of comparisons make it easier to see the particular strengths of entrepreneurial leadership, such as creativity or persistence in problem-solving, resource procurement, and partnership-building. Entrepreneurial leadership seems to be a prerequisite for adaptive change, but not all entrepreneurs are equally skilled in leading people through the change. One potential pitfall of this kind of leadership is anti-democratic behavior.

Entrepreneurial leadership is not often associated with public education. However, in one study of elementary school principals in Israel, the teachers reported that 56 percent of the leaders were more or less entrepreneurial. That's pretty good. However, only 11 percent were real out-of-the-box thinkers, so there is room for improvement.

There would be no point in writing this book unless one believed that all leaders can learn to be more entrepreneurial. There is some evidence that proven entrepreneurial leaders can get better at what they do. The case study of the early college program showcased some opportunistic leaders who worked together to develop a more radical, frame-breaking innovation. The next chapter explores ways in which organizations can support entrepreneurial leadership.

## NOTES

1. See, for example: Borasi, R., & Finnigan, K. (2010). Entrepreneurial attitudes and behaviors that can help prepare successful change-agents in education. *New Educator, 6*(1), 1–29.

2. Perhaps "they are not heroic figures, but rather, 'career' professionals or experienced social economy actors." Humbert, A. L. (2012). *Women as social entrepreneurs* (p. 6). Birmingham, UK: Third Sector Research Centre, quoting Amin (2009).

3. *Oxford English Dictionary.* (2010). New York: Oxford University Press.

4. Dees, J. G. (1998). *The meaning of "social entrepreneurship"* (p. 6). Kansas City, KS: Kauffman Center for Entrepreneurial Leadership.

5. Trofimov, I. D. (2012). The failure of the International Trade Organization (ITO): A policy entrepreneurship perspective. *Journal of Politics and Law, 5*(1), 56–68.

6. Schumpeter, J. (1934). *The theory of economic development: An inquiry into profits, capital, credit, interest, and the business cycle.* Cambridge, MA: Harvard University Press.

7. Schumpeter, J. (1942). *Capitalism, socialism and democracy* (p. 83). New York: Harper and Brothers.

8. Malcolm Gladwell, who delights in upending common assumptions, established this fact. Gladwell, M. (2010). The sure thing: How entrepreneurs really succeed. *New Yorker, 86*(3), 24–29.

9. Kirzner, I. (1973). *Competition and entrepreneurship.* Chicago, IL: University of Chicago Press.

10. Trofimov, I. D., 63.

11. Martin, R. L., & Osberg, S. (2007). Social entrepreneurship: The case for definition. *Stanford Social Innovation Review, 5*(2), 28–39.

12. Craig, J., Green, M., & Johnson, D. (2004). *Classifying entrepreneurs as Schumpeterian (innovator-entrepreneur) versus Kirznerian (producer-entrepreneur).* Paper presented at the Frontiers of Entrepreneurship Research: Proceedings of the Twenty-Fourth Annual Entrepreneurship Research Conference, Babson Park, MA.

13. Trofimov, I. D.

14. Drayton, B. (2007, November 28). Good Q&A: Bill Drayton, para. 2. Retrieved September 27, 2012, from http://www.good.is/posts/good_qa_bill_drayton/.

15. Dacin, P. A., Dacin, M. T., & Matear, M. (2010). Social entrepreneurship: Why we don't need a new theory and how we move forward from here. *Academy of Management Perspectives, 24*(3), 37–57.

16. Mair, J., & Martí, I. (2006). Social entrepreneurship research: A source of explanation, prediction, and delight. *Journal of World Business, 41*(1), 36–44.

17. Yunus, M. (2003). *Banker to the poor: Microlending and the battle against world poverty.* New York: Public Affairs.

18. Bornstein, D. (2004). *How to change the world: Social entrepreneurs and the power of new ideas.* New York: Oxford University Press.

19. Mair, J., & Martí, I.

20. Williams, E. E., & Findlay, M. C., III (1981). A reconsideration of the rationality postulate: "Right hemisphere thinking" in economics. *American Journal of Economics & Sociology, 40*(1), 20.

21. Chen, J. (2013, February 1). Should your business be nonprofit or for-profit? Retrieved from http://blogs.hbr.org/cs/2013/02/should_your_business_be_nonpro.html.

22. Sometimes called "public sector entrepreneurs," as in Boyett, I. (1996). The public sector entrepreneur—a definition. *International Journal of Public Sector Management, 9*(2).

23. Austin, J., Stevenson, H., & Wei-Skillern, J. (2011). Social and commercial entrepreneurship: Same, different, or both? *Revista de Administração, 47*(3), 370–384. doi: http://dx.doi.org/10.1590/S0080-21072012000300003.

24. Dees, J. G.

25. Mair, J., & Martí, I.

26. Hodgson, D. C. (2012, June 2). Social entrepreneurship soars as a career choice: Finding meaning in work and life, para. 10. Retrieved from http://www.huffingtonpost.com/david-c-hodgson/social-entrepreneurship-career-choice_b_1562949.html.

27. Dees, J. G., 3.

28. Dacin, P. A., Dacin, M. T., & Matear, M.; Hoogendoorn, B., Pennings, E., & Thurik, R. (2011). A conceptual overview of what we know about social entrepreneurship. In J. DeFilippes & S. Saegert (Eds.), *The Community Development Reader* (p. 15). New York: Routledge; Martin, R. L., & Osberg, S.; Zahra, S. A., Gedajlovic, E., Neubaum, D. O., & Shulman, J. M. (2009). A typology of social entrepreneurs: Motives, search processes and ethical challenges. *Journal of Business Venturing, 24*(5), 519–532.

29. Hoogendoorn, B., Pennings, E., & Thurik, R.

30. Martin, R. L., & Osberg, S.

31. Zahra, S. A., Gedajlovic, E., Neubaum, D. O., & Shulman, J. M.

32. Dacin, P. A., Dacin, M. T., & Matear, M.

33. Martin, R. L., & Osberg, S.

34. Zahra, S. A., Gedajlovic, E., Neubaum, D. O., & Shulman, J. M.

35. TEDxRochester (Producer). (2010, November 1). Warner School of Education– University of Rochester. [videoclip]. Retrieved from http://www.facebook.com/warner.school/posts/178926722161230.

36.  Mair, J., & Martí, I.

37.  Zahra, S. A., Gedajlovic, E., Neubaum, D. O., & Shulman, J. M.

38.  Werter, L. Y. (2011). *Has someone seen my spark? Entrepreneurship in Oxfam Novib.* Master's degree thesis, Universiteit Utrecht, Utrecht, p. 22. Retrieved from http://igitur-archive.library.uu.nl/student-theses/2011-1118-200806/UUindex.html.

39.  Feir, R. E. (1995). *National patterns of state education policy innovation and three deviant cases*, p. 31. Paper presented at the annual meeting of the American Educational Research Association, San Francisco, CA.

40.  Boyett, I.

41.  Lavaroni, C. W., & Leisey, D. E. An open letter to California school board members. Retrieved May 8, 2010, from http://www.edentrepreneurs.org/.

42.  Pinchot, G., III. (1985). *Intrapreneuring: Why you don't have to leave the corporation to become an entrepreneur.* New York: Harper & Row.

43.  Carrier, C. (1996). Intrapreneurship in small businesses: An exploratory study. *Entrepreneurship: Theory & Practice, 21*(1), 5–20.

44.  For more on this kind of entrepreneur, see Brown, R. J., & Cornwall, J. R. (Eds.). (2000). *The entrepreneurial educator.* Lanham, MD: Scarecrow Education; Cornwall, J. R. (2003). *From the ground up: Entrepreneurial school leadership.* Lanham, MD: Scarecrow Education; Hess, F. M. (Ed.). (2006). *Educational entrepreneurship: Realities, challenges, possibilities.* Cambridge, MA: Harvard Education Press; Hess, F. M. (Ed.). (2008). *The future of educational entrepreneurship: Possibilities for school reform.* Cambridge, MA: Harvard Education Press.

45.  For an exception to this trend, see Humbert, A. L.

46.  Bornstein, D., xii–xiii.

47.  Humbert, A. L.

48.  Humbert, A. L.

49.  Goleman, D. (2000). Leadership that gets results. *Harvard Business Review, 78*(2), 78–90.

50.  Goleman, D., 78.

51.  Eyal, O., & Kark, R. (2004). How do transformational leaders transform organizations? A study of the relationship between leadership and entrepreneurship. *Leadership and Policy in Schools, 3*(3), 215.

52.  Mair, J., & Martí, I.

53.  Borasi, R., & Finnigan, K.

54.  Burns, J. M. (1978). *Leadership.* New York: Harper & Row.

55.  Burns, J. M., 4.

56.  Bass, B. M., & Avolio, B. J. (Eds.). (1994). *Improving organizational effectiveness through transformational leadership.* Thousand Oaks, CA: Sage Publications.

57.  Eyal, O., & Kark, R., 228.

58.  Eyal, O., & Kark, R., 221.

59.  Spillane, J. (2006). *Distributed leadership.* San Francisco, CA: Jossey-Bass; Spillane, J., Halverson, R., & Diamond, J. (2004). Towards a theory of

leadership practice: A distributed perspective. *Journal of Curriculum Studies, 36*(1), 3–34.

60. Heifetz, R. A., & Laurie, D. L. (1997). The work of leadership. *Harvard Business Review, 75*(1), 124–134; Heifetz, R. A., & Linsky, M. (2002). *Leadership on the line: Staying alive through the dangers of leading.* Boston: Harvard Business School Press.

61. Heifetz, R. A., & Linsky, M., 19.

62. Fullan, M. (1993). *Change forces: Probing the depths of educational reform* (p. 25). London: Falmer Press.

63. Heifetz, R. A., & Linsky, M., 127.

64. Fullan, M. (2001). *Leading in a culture of change* (p. 38). San Francisco: Jossey-Bass.

65. Marzano, R. J., Waters, T., & McNulty, B. A. (2005). *School leadership that works: From research to results* (p. 68). Alexandria, VA: Association for Supervisors and Curriculum Development.

66. Eyal, O., & Inbar, D. E. (2003). Developing a public school entrepreneurship inventory: Theoretical conceptualization and empirical examination. *International Journal of Entrepreneurial Behaviour and Research, 9*(6), 221–244.

67. Eyal, O., & Kark, R., 221.

68. Eyal, O., & Kark, R., 222.

69. Eyal, O., & Inbar, D. E.

70. Eyal, O., & Kark, R., 214.

71. Eyal, O., & Kark, R., 214–5.

72. Eyal, O., & Kark, R., 215.

73. Eyal, O., & Kark, R., 215.

74. Eyal, O., & Inbar, D. E., 235.

75. Eyal, O., & Kark, R., 215.

76. Eyal, O., & Inbar, D. E., 235.

77. Leonard, J. (2010). *Taking dual enrollment deeper: Supports for the "forgotten middle" in a tenth grade classroom.* Paper presented at the American Educational Research Association, Denver, CO.

78. Sperling, C. (2009). *The Massachusetts community colleges developmental education best policy and practice audit: Final report.* Boston: Massachusetts Community Colleges Executive Office.

79. Hoffman, N., & Vargas, J. (2005). *Integrating grades 9 through 14: State policies to support and sustain early college high schools. Early college high school initiative* (p. 20). Boston, MA: Jobs for the Future; Webb, M. (2004). *What is the cost of planning and implementing early college high school?* (p. 46). Boston, MA: Jobs for the Future; Zehr, M. A. (2010, December 20). Cutbacks force some early colleges to close down. *Education Week.* Retrieved from http://www.edweek.org/ew/articles/2010/12/20/15earlycollege_ep.h30.html.

80. Leonard, J. (2013a). Funding early college high school: Hold harmless or shared commitment. *Education Policy Analysis Archives, 13*(46). http://epaa.aju.edu/ojs/article/view/1214.

81. Karp, M. M., Calcagno, J. C., Hughes, K. L., Jeong, D. W., & Bailey, T. R. (2007). *The postsecondary achievement of participants in dual enrollment: "An analysis of student outcomes in two states"* (C. U. Community College Research Center, Trans.): National Research Center for Career and Technical Education.

82. Adelman, C. (2006). *The toolbox revisited: Paths to degree completion from high school through college* (p. xx). Washington, DC: US Department of Education.

83. Leonard, J. (2013b). Maximizing college readiness for all through parental support. *School Community Journal*, 23(1), 183–202.

84. Leonard, J. (2013a).

85. Leonard, J. (2013c). *Using ecological systems theory to support college readiness*. Paper presented at the annual convention of the American Educational Research Association, San Francisco.

86. Borasi, R., & Finnigan, K., 21.

# 3

# ENTREPRENEURIAL ORGANIZATIONS

"What we've done to encourage innovation is make it ordinary."[1]

In the 1980s a Harvard professor named Rosabeth Moss Kanter wrote a classic on intrapreneurship called *The Change Masters*.[2] She studied over one hundred large corporations, personally visiting fifty of them and performing an in-depth study of ten, while tracking the progress of 115 innovations at these target companies. Kanter used employee metaphors in this description of the organizational culture of one vibrant, innovative company:

> Employees portrayed [their work place] with a variety of vivid images: a family, a competing guild, a society on a secluded Pacific island, a group of people with an organization chart hung around it, a gypsy society, a university, a theocracy, twenty-five different companies, and a company with "ten thousand entrepreneurs."[3]

Imagine the public school district in your city or town. To what extent would creative metaphors such as these ever apply? Chapter 2 hinted that really powerful entrepreneurship is sometimes more an organizational phenomenon than the fruit of one talented leader. Cutting-edge companies deliberately cultivate an alternative culture that encourages experimentation and new ideas.

Chapter 2 introduced the social entrepreneur, who serves the public good, and the intrapreneur, who innovates within a larger institution—the two most common characteristics of most K–12 entrepreneurs. This chapter considers organizational characteristics that encourage them. Rather than looking specifically at the talented innovator, the focus shifts to the context and environment in which they work. Beginning with a quick assessment of the prevailing culture in public education, the discussion moves to leadership behaviors that help or hinder entrepreneurial activity and then the organizational characteristics of really innovative enterprises.

Chapter 1 suggested that the presence of safety lines, like the belaying lines that protect rock climbers, can reduce the risk and provide a safe environment for learning and growth. There is a difference between safety lines and binding cords. In this age of accountability, there is a strong temptation to predetermine educational outcomes by micromanaging with rules that disallow distractions or deviations. The multiplication of central office rules and requirements can swamp and exhaust staff members, discourage reflection and inventiveness, and extinguish innovative thinking. Safety lines make it safe to experiment, while accountability threats can shut down creativity. Somehow, there is a need for more safety lines and fewer binding ropes.

There is little doubt that current structures and leadership practices are hindering entrepreneurism in education. Recall the California researchers in chapter 1 who could not find a single district that had a program in place to identify, encourage, and support entrepreneurially minded leaders.[4] Instead, the entrepreneurially minded leaders were leaving public education for service in other organizations where they were free to imagine.

Ken Kay, the retiring president of the Partnership for 21st Century Skills reinforced this image of public education when he wrote,

> I went around the country and met with thirty district superintendents. . . . *None* of those superintendents felt that federal or state policy was helping their efforts to innovate. This perception was reinforced last spring when I participated in *Education Week*'s "Innovation InSight" events in New York and Chicago. When I asked about two hundred practitioners whether state policy was supporting their efforts to innovate, not one person raised a hand. When I asked if federal policy was supporting their efforts to innovate, only one person raised her hand. We have a huge disconnect in this country: State and federal policymakers think they are innovating, but they are not partnering with or supporting the efforts of the most innovative districts in our country.[5]

This is a problem. The beginning of this book discussed the tremendous interest in innovation in education and some of the federal and state programs which have been rolled out in support of this creativity. However, people on the ground such as Ken Kay do not feel the same support.

Another example contrasts New York City's innovative in-district principal preparation program with the prevailing culture of the larger district. The fresh leaders were recruited and trained to lead their schools in new directions, but they found a different reality when they began to work within the enormous city bureaucracy, reporting that "they felt like second-class citizens in their schools and were even set up to fail by administrators who had little interest in seeing them succeed."[6] An innovative plan for new school leadership that came from one department in the district was quashed by animosity and indifference from other sectors.

There are hundreds of books that offer guidance to aspiring entrepreneurs. Less common are those that address the entrepreneurs buried within organizations—the intrapreneurs—although scholars were writing about this topic as early as the 1980s.[7] Some of those lessons are just beginning to be applied to public education.

## LEADING FOR INNOVATION

One of the most important facts about leadership in innovative organizations is that the leader is often not the innovator. This can be a hard lesson for leaders if they are used to being at the forefront of everything.[8] For example, two highly creative teachers left the traditional school system and started their own charter school where they could forefront the beliefs and practices that proved most effective in their classrooms. They completed the definition of entrepreneurial leadership offered in chapter 1: taking an idea from conception and turning it into an enterprise, which had intellectual and social value. Predictably, they were soon swamped with the management challenges of a new organization and the creative work on innovation was taken up by other teachers within the school.

In the business and engineering worlds, great inventions tend to emerge from the ranks. With this in mind, Kouzes and Posner wrote, "The leader's major contributions are in the creation of a climate for experimentation, the recognition of good ideas, the support of these ideas, and the willingness to challenge the system to get new products, processes, services, and systems adopted."[9] This is all part of the process of creating a safe environment where nascent ideas can learn to walk and grow up.

Some leadership behaviors are decidedly counter-productive. Tongue-in-cheek, Kanter listed some rules for stifling innovation:[10]

- Regard any idea from below with suspicion.[11]
- Treat identification of problems as a sign of failure.[12]
- Invoke history. If a new idea comes up for discussion, find a precedent in an earlier idea that didn't work and remind everyone of that bad past experience.[13]
- Keep people really busy. If people seem to have free time, load them with more work.[14]
- In the name of excellence, encourage cut-throat competition. Get groups to critique and challenge each other's proposals, preferably in public forums, and then declare winners and losers.[15]
- Express your criticisms freely and withhold your praise.[16] Act as though punishing failure motivates success. Practice public humiliation, making object lessons out of those who fail to meet expectations. Everyone will know that risk-taking is bad.[17]
- Control everything carefully. Make sure people count anything that can be counted, frequently.[18]
- Make decisions to reorganize or change policies in secret and spring them on people unexpectedly.[19] This ensures that no one will start anything new because they never know what new orders will be coming down from the top.[20]
- Make sure that requests for information are fully justified, and make sure that it is not given out . . . freely.[21]
- Above all, never forget that we got to the top because we already know everything there is to know about this business.[22]

These practices are sadly commonplace in many large organizations, including public education. This kind of leadership will never lead to innovative cultures in K–12 education or anywhere else.

Some strategies for entrepreneurial thinking have limited effectiveness, such as the top-down dictate where innovation is ordered in a command-and-control organization.[23] Innovation in a compliance atmosphere is an oxymoron. Teresa Amabile of the Harvard Business School has studied the preconditions and components of creativity as they apply to the business world as well as public education. According to her, creativity of every kind, including entrepreneurial creativity, is considered to be the result of three things that come together: knowledge related to the field of endeavor, creative thinking strategies, and intrinsic task motivation.[24] The need for some baseline knowledge goes without saying. For example, one would be hard-pressed to improve on the gasoline engine without first having an understanding of how engines work.

There are numerous strategies for creative thinking—the second component—which can be learned and should be taught more often.

Some of these will be taken up in later chapters, but three are worth mentioning here. First, creative people are comfortable in disagreeing with others—not just to be disagreeable but to consider alternative ideas. Secondly, they make it a habit to entertain alternative solutions. And finally, while creative people (and entrepreneurs) can be obsessive about their work, they also have no qualms about walking away so they can come back later with a fresh perspective.[25] One can see that these creative habits would be harder to maintain in a busy command-and-control organization.

The last component of creativity is motivation, for little is produced when people are unmotivated. Some American school districts try to incentivize successful teachers with additional pay. Some districts publish teachers' names alongside student achievement test results in the newspaper. While the subject of incentives is further developed later in this chapter, there is ample research to demonstrate that these positive and negative extrinsic motivators are detrimental to risk-taking, experimentation, and, of course, creativity and innovation. In contrast, there are some extrinsic motivators that can support creativity, such as the offer of material support or vital information, which will facilitate the creative process.[26]

For the most part, creative people are motivated intrinsically by the challenge, the joy of creating, and personal interest. Chapter 1 suggested that they have a high internal locus of control and attribute their success to their own efforts rather than to external circumstances. Furthermore, they simply love what they are doing. Lynn Gatto, the enterprising elementary school teacher described in chapter 1, is a good example. As she confessed,

> It's like living in a dysfunctional family, and no one can really keep tabs on you; so for someone who is highly motivated, knows how to teach, knows what to do, this is a wonderful place to work because I can just tool along.[27]

Sometimes, innovation occurs despite the organizational culture because there are holes or hidden areas in the organization.[28] Later, this chapter will consider the loosely coupled nature of most K–12 districts, which provides teachers such as Gatto with an opportunity for entrepreneurial innovation.

People who are given to creative, entrepreneurial thinking do not require very much since they are intrinsically motivated; for the most part, they just want to be left alone. However, there are many extrinsic factors and misguided motivators that can squelch this kind of thinking. The question remains: how can a government bureaucracy move from being an anti-entrepreneurial institution to one that actively supports and encourages innovation?

Large institutions will often try to encourage innovation with a few hothouse pilot projects.[29] Pilots sometimes need more than one leader to promote and protect the entrepreneurism from the larger environment. Scott described four important roles in large enterprises.[30] The intrapreneur with the original spark is called the *idea champion*. A second kind of leader is the *sponsor*, who serves as an ally, promoting the new idea so it gains a listening ear. The *godfather* is a more powerful leader who can carve out political space for the idea and ensure that it is not extinguished. Finally, other leaders create a *greenhouse* where the innovation is sealed off from the rest of the firm and can grow to fruition. Together, these leaders help create an organizational setting that encourages entrepreneurism.

Pilot projects can backfire, however, by cornering innovation rather than releasing it.[31] One large American city, for example, launched a dozen pilot schools in the 1990s where many of the central office and union contracting rules were relaxed so principals would have more discretion in regard to budgeting, staffing, scheduling, curriculum, and governance. The pilot schools often had a longer school year, longer days, smaller classes, more technology, more support, and, significantly, they had longer waiting lists for students.[32]

The pilots were largely successful for those students fortunate enough to gain a seat, but the practices proven successful in the pilots did not spread easily across the district. The successes were isolated. Other principals complained bitterly that they were pitted against the pilots and losing students in the city's school choice program even as their own hands were tied with rules that the pilots could ignore. In this situation, innovation was limited and even resented by those who could not participate.

A second misguided route to innovation can be the outside expert, brought in to solve thorny company problems. Not all consultants are bad; if the school or district plans on growing in a new direction, such as the adoption of a new curriculum or a switch to central office accounting systems, then new leadership is essential.[33] But, sometimes, an expert is hired for the wrong reasons. As chapter 1 demonstrated, an urgent need in organizational reform is for adaptive thinking where the difficult learning work is done by those inside the organization. Technical solutions, such as hiring an expert, are temporary, and the core, institutional problems will soon resurface. Hiring an outside consultant can be doubly debilitating when it relieves the insiders of this work and conveys cultural inferiority. The subtle message is that no one inside the organization has a good idea or the motivation to make changes.

There are positive leadership behaviors that will encourage organizational entrepreneurism. The leadership behaviors described in the following lie on a spectrum from least active to the most active interventions. The most obvious approach to unleashing entrepreneurism is to get out of the way. So, for example, one San Diego superintendent "ruled that no central office middle managers reject an innovative plan proposed by a school."[34] This ensured that innovations would have time to develop and gain an ear with top leadership.

Getting out of the way is a disarmingly easy step. One might think that innovators need all kinds of props and supports, but, in fact, one of their top wishes is that management would just leave them alone. Entrepreneurs will do what they do regardless of the obstacles. Getting out of the way is not the same as indifference. The paragraphs below describe various degrees of minimalist leadership that signal support without stifling innovation.

Leadership for adaptive learning is the kind of leadership required in organizations that want to promote creative, inventive, out-of-the-box thinking, new solutions, and cutting-edge innovations. This can sometimes mean doing nothing as the leader steps out of the way and declines to divert attention from the problem. Such leadership runs contrary to heroic instincts that want to run to the rescue, provide answers, and show the path forward. In fact, do-nothing leadership can spark resentment and accusations. Nevertheless, these are often the dire circumstances that spark up-from-the-ranks initiative, inventiveness, and learning.

Leadership through adaptive challenges exercises calculated restraint, offering isolated observations, using parsimonious questioning, and taking action only when the learning process gets completely stalled. In comparison to common portrayals of dynamic leadership, this is minimal leadership. Every step toward getting on top of the process risks sabotaging the process.

Canadian researcher Camille Carrier studied intrapreneurship in five small businesses of two hundred employees or less, in contrast to the large corporations studied by Kanter.[35] The small size afforded her a close look at leadership behaviors. She found that leaders who promoted intrapreneurship had to be "able to delegate to and have confidence in their employees."[36] This was different from the getting-out-of-the-way approach described previously. Leaders who delegate are still setting the vision and determining what needs to be done; however, when they limit their contribution to direction-setting and leave the figuring-out-how-to-get-there work to others, they leave the door open for innovative solutions.

Other scholars stress the importance of sharing resources and information to support entrepreneurism.[37] Sharing information invites vulnerability but also solutions. For example, school leaders can be tight-fisted when it comes to sharing student achievement data, even with their own staff. Some of this stems from federal regulations that protect student privacy, but there are simple ways to anonymize the data. Too often, the reluctance to share can be traced back to other motives, such as leadership insecurity or insufficient time to prepare and protect the data. Data analysis is central to school improvement, and the more hands involved, the better. There is no good excuse for hoarding.

Researchers also list "enabling behaviors" that leaders can use to enhance innovative thinking.[38] They describe a "cheerleading" environment where "the myths, stories, approved vocabulary, rules, and rituals of the corporation stress creative rather than conventional behaviors."[39] Everybody wants more entrepreneurial leadership in schools these days, but the leadership behaviors and organizational climate often speak otherwise.

Enabling behaviors are better caught than taught; the leader must model true approval and support in repeated encounters with teachers and administrators. Ken Kay (quoted earlier in this chapter) believed that top education leaders needed to be more careful to identify the innovators within their ranks and highlight their work. This is one way of creating the myths and rituals that stress creative behaviors. He also believed innovators should be deliberately invited to top-level policy deliberations.[40] As Kay admitted, this seems like a small step, but it is fundamental to signaling an open ear to fresh ideas. If the creative solutions for tough urban schools are sitting right at hand, then a simple signal like this could make a big difference.

Social learning theory offers important lessons for leaders who want an entrepreneurial organization. For example, entrepreneurial thinkers have a high sense of self-efficacy. Albert Bandura identified four sources of self-efficacy.[41] Leaders can use social persuasion (cheerleading) to increase the self-efficacy of their staff members. They can also model the behaviors, such as innovativeness, that they want to encourage. The exercise of entrepreneurism is contagious. When workers perceive that their leader is bold, creative, and willing to take risks, they are more likely to express the same characteristics. The leader sets the tone for the organization.

Self-efficacy for a particular behavior, such as entrepreneurism, also increases with mastery practice. This was Bandura's third suggestion. Time must be set aside if one hopes to achieve mastery in any skill, including innovativeness, so Kanter recommended slack time for experimentation.[42] Of course, practice implies failure, so leaders must make room for mistakes. A second leadership behavior that Carrier found in the small businesses was "tolerating failure by granting the right to fail to anyone willing to risk adopting a different approach."[43]

School teachers are often afraid to experiment with new instructional methods, especially in high-stakes accountability environments such as turnaround schools. Michael Fung's forgiveness sticks, described in chapter 1, are one way to reduce the threat of failure. Some school leaders encourage experimentation by negotiating the supervision and evaluation process. The teachers inform their principal when they want to experiment with a new curriculum or instructional strategy, and the principal agrees to observe and provide feedback, while removing the experiment from the evaluation process.

Bandura also determined that self-efficacy concepts were related to one's emotional and psychological state. High levels of stress, for example, could undermine self-efficacy. Subsequent chapters will consider the role of social networking, down-time, cross-sector exploration, and even reading as important factors in building a high sense of self-efficacy and entrepreneurial thinking. Creative people understand the importance of walking away from a problem so one can return with a fresh perspective. Educational leaders who want innovative teams need to consider these tips.

Not all leaders are entrepreneurial, but they can lead innovative organizations. Pinchot insisted,

> The corporate officers and staffs of successful large organizations will increasingly see their roles shift from one of telling others what to do to that of creating the rules by which free people in their organizations can perform on their own inspiration.[44]

## ORGANIZATIONAL CHARACTERISTICS

Many researchers call entrepreneurship an "organization-level phenomenon," which implies that it is less about one inspired leader and more about an organizational framework that promotes entrepreneurism.[45] There are many reasons to believe that organizational characteristics are better predictors of entrepreneurial activity. Innovation often emerges from the ranks, sometimes without the knowledge or support of the top leaders, so the organizational culture should be considered.

Carrier described organizational characteristics that enhanced or hindered intrapreneurial energy.[46] For example, organizational structures that were flatter, with fewer hierarchical layers, reduced the number of obstacles between the budding idea and the owner-manager who could provide information and resources. Secondly, an organizational culture that was less formal made it easier to gain an ear and find recognition.

Territoriality can be a terrible hindrance to innovation. Many educators are familiar with the territorial tendencies of big school districts, where separate departments that address budgets, human resources, technology, content specialties, special education, or English acquisition can resemble fiefdoms with closely guarded information and contradictory policies. For boundary-spanning entrepreneurs, who tend to think holistically, this kind of structure can be perplexing and prohibitive.

In her research on large corporations in the 1980s, Kanter differentiated two kinds of organizational cultures. Segmentalist companies practiced compartmentalization. Structurally, they were dense hierarchies with multiple divisions and departments. They approached problems compartmentally, believing that "problems can be solved when they are carved into pieces and the pieces are assigned to specialists who work in isolation."[47] Problems were often seen as a threat or an embarrassment and were addressed in private. There was little communication across boundaries and knowledge was not shared. In a segmentalist organization, no one had "any real information about upper management thinking."[48]

In contrast, innovative companies were characterized by an integrative culture, where knowledge was freely shared intra-organizationally. These companies saw problems as opportunities, as healthy challenges to established practice. They approached problems as a whole, in their context, with the attention of the entire corporation, rather than piecemeal in isolation. Furthermore, innovative companies had often replaced the traditional ladder-like hierarchical structure with a matrix-like organizational chart. Some leaders might have accountability in multiple directions, thus increasing teamwork and communication. Permanent departments ran parallel with fluid, temporary "ad-hocracies," such as project teams and "professional self-managed work teams."[49]

In the innovative companies, Kanter found a leadership style known as "management-by-walking-around" where management was visibly present and accessible and small problems could be addressed on the spot in real time.[50] There was "a remarkable open-mindedness—willingness to listen, nondefensiveness, and ability to let go of an investment in their own ideas in order to pick up on a different idea that might produce results."[51] Innovation was not assigned as the business of one division or relegated to a small team of designated entrepreneurs. Instead, innovation was the business of the entire company; the entire company was geared to experiment, to test ideas, and to disturb and challenge the status quo. Similarly, Eyal and Kark described an "organizational *consensus* to overcome internal resistance that might hinder the implementation of the innovations."[52]

Kanter's description of segmentalist and integrative cultures should not be confused with Weick's research on loosely and tightly coupled organizations.[53] Whereas Kanter looked at the arrangement of the parts (hierarchical versus matrix-like, for example), Weick looked at the integrity of processes between the parts. His theory is equally informative, however, when it comes to understanding the conditions conducive to innovation.

Weick viewed school systems as loosely coupled organizations because elements within the organization—the teachers, leaders, and schools themselves—retained some of their own identity despite organizational pressures to conform. The transfer of information was less than perfect. So, for example, a district-wide reading initiative would be implemented inconsistently across the district as it was interpreted differently from school to school. Differences in implementation could even be found between classrooms within the same school. In contrast, the United States Army would be a tightly coupled organization, where individual identity is less preserved and orders are more faithfully carried out. Coupling defines the transfer process.

Weick speculated that schools persisted as loosely coupled organizations (despite numerous efforts to tighten the coupling) because this was cost-effective and the ramifications of looseness were not serious.[54] There are advantages to loose coupling. Such organizations tend to be more sensitive to the local environment, so teachers are in a front-row seat to accurately assess student needs and respond creatively. Surely, this is healthy for students.

Loose coupling also increases adaptability, since the individual elements (teachers or schools) enjoy more independence and can respond to local conditions. This has obvious implications for adaptive learning, which is so central to the work of schools. The experimental process of trial and error, being local, is less costly. Mistakes do not reverberate across the district. Neither do successes, however. The lack of information transfer fidelity means that successful innovations may not spread to other classrooms or schools.

Loosely coupled organizations are definitely more innovative. Weick found that these kinds of organizations were more improvisational than planned and more accommodative than constrained.[55] But, there is a second problem with loose coupling:

> Frequent local adjustments, unconstrained by centralized policy, keep small problems from amplifying. If major change becomes nec-

essary, however, it is much harder to diffuse it among systems that are loosely coupled. Loosely coupled systems reduce the necessity for large-scale change but also make it more difficult to achieve if it is needed.[56]

Sometimes, large-scale changes are imperative, especially when the rights of children are being violated. The challenge, then, is how to retain the innovative benefits of loose coupling while not obstructing whole-scale change when it becomes necessary. This has been the story of recent years, as the nationalization of the American school system has led to a tightening of national standards and regional accountability systems.

There is a need for deep and continuous change within the American public educational system. According to Weick, a loosely coupled system is ideal for local, environmentally sensitive innovation and, furthermore, reduces the need for major changes because change is continuous.[57] However, when large-scale change is needed, loosely coupled systems are resistant. The information is not transferred faithfully. The vestiges of nineteenth-century educational practices that stubbornly persist in the face of twenty-first-century demographics, technological advances, and globalization beg for major change. Furthermore, when there are promising innovations at the local level, they are not easily transmitted across the system. How can one promote major change without destroying this local, entrepreneurial innovativeness?

Kanter suggested that the integrative culture is most appropriate in the middle layers of the organization and that the middle managers would most profit from matrix-type relationships.[58] In school systems, the top layer belongs to the superintendent's team, and the lowest layer consists of the school children. Middle management means the principal and the teachers. Kanter claimed that initiative among this group would be "encouraged by a combination of relative independence from higher levels and relative interdependence among peers across functions."[59] This is a model for schooling that is still only partially appreciated.

Louis and Miles described four kinds of relationships between districts and individual schools, which they discovered in their research on effective school reform.[60] In contrast to an evolutionary planning strategy, professional development strategy, or top-down implementation strategy, the authors found that a goal-based accountability strategy allowed the district to specify paramount goals, while leaving the details of process and implementation to the schools. For example, a district could specify that all schools must make adequate yearly progress according to the federally mandated accountability system, but they would individually be free to select the schedule, teachers, and curriculum best designed to achieve that goal. The "interdependence among peers" of the matrix organization would be reflected in teacher teams who examine student data, brainstorm solutions, and share innovative ideas and practices.[61]

Interdependence does make for slower decisions, which can be frustrating, and a matrix-like table of organization can leave one wondering, at times, who is in charge. One manager told Kanter, "The matrix left us begging for someone to make a decision."[62] This may not sound inviting to the average principal, but the alternative is an army-like command-and-control structure, which few school leaders enjoy. "Begging for a decision" is the invitation to adaptive learning, which is the companion of entrepreneurial innovativeness.

## DISCRETION

There is not a single cookbook recipe for a successful school. Classroom teachers must respond to diverse learners even as the external political and economic environment changes from year to year. A practice that works so well in one school can sometimes fall short in another school; promising practices can even fail from one year to the next. Therefore, the need to experiment and respond creatively never ends. Faced with this uncertainty, local educators are best served by a combination of "provider discretion and performance accountability."[63] In other words, principals and teachers need the freedom to make important decisions within a framework of external accountability. Discretion is the prerequisite for entrepreneurial innovation.

There is a difference between compliance and accountability. The former says, "You must do it this way" even when there is a better, more efficient way to reach the same end. When the Department of Motor Vehicles asks a customer to update an automobile registration every few years to ensure adequate insurance coverage for public safety, that is accountability. When the DMV requires the customer appear in person to renew the registration, even though an online application could serve the same purpose at considerable savings, that is just compliance. Of course, accountability goes both ways. The DMV must be accountable to enforce the same rules and to provide a fair and efficient service for a fee. The key is to maximize discretion while preserving accountability for the public good.

Accountability is more complicated in a matrix, when both horizontal and vertical relationships demand attention. Learning to lead in an integrative environment with matrix-like lines of accountability is not easy. Kanter estimated that it required "about three to five years for a manager to learn to work within the matrix."[64] The shifting structure calls for responsibility in multiple directions and requires, at the same time, proactivity and decisiveness.

The complexity of the matrix-like structure in the middle layers of the organization need not be replicated above or below. In fact, at the top layers of the organization—the superintendent's office—Kanter recommended "the stability and simplicity of focused plans."[65] This is a combination that answers to the need for major change without destroying local inventiveness. The district carves out broad goals and then leaves the strategies, the solutions, and the adaptive learning in the hands of the middle managers.

When there is a different organizational structure in the middle and top of an organization, then different kinds of leaders are required. Educators who are inclined to be entrepreneurial might be most rewarded at the mid-levels of an organization where discretion is maximized. For many reasons, the superintendent's office is a hard place for a James Dean, break-all-the-rules rebel to operate.

## PROFESSIONAL LEARNING COMMUNITIES

Teacher leadership and professional learning communities are recent steps toward a more integrative organizational structure in public schools. Educators have long bemoaned the isolation of teachers in separate, nineteenth-century classrooms where closed doors hinder sharing best practices and peer mentoring. In recent years, changes in scheduling and even space configurations have made professional learning communities—or PLCs—possible, where teachers can meet weekly to learn from one another.[66] This is the seedbed for adaptive learning, where the people who have the problem must be the ones who do the learning work.[67]

The benefits of PLCs will be explored more in chapter 5. However, the same idea was widely promoted in the business literature so many years earlier. William Ouchi described work groups called "quality circles" in 1982 , which were designed to encourage honest discussion, questioning, skepticism, and refinements of the work; mutual trust was the primary outcome.[68] In the same decade, Deal and Kennedy described a "productive work ecology, in which flexible work units are linked in the corporate whole like molecules, transforming and dissolving as problems emerge and are resolved."[69] This is exactly the integrative approach described by Kanter that was so vital for intrapreneurship.

Despite this knowledge, which has been around for over thirty years, and the recent emphasis on professional learning communities, a 2009 survey of American teachers demonstrated that teachers still spend 93 percent of their time alone, collaborating only 2.7 hours per week on average.[70] The situation with school principals is equally dire, for they find little opportunity to meet and, when they do, they are often saddled with district- and state-mandated professional development agendas. In this environment, there is little incentive to collaborate. Most teachers and principals grew up in segmentalist schools, were likely trained in segmentalist universities, and began their careers in segmentalist districts. Without a radical reorientation, they are unlikely to think outside the boundaries and significant innovation will be limited.

## PROXIMITY

The professional learning community concept is not without its critics, for in some cases the meetings are driven with top-down agendas that continue to stifle reflection and creative thinking. In short, they become just another manifestation of a top-down, command-and-control culture. What is not appreciated is that face-to-face contact in an unscheduled format can encourage the sharing and dissemination of best practices and also stimulate the invention of new ideas and superior approaches.

The organizational conditions for innovative thinking can sometimes be physical. In other words, proximity appears to promote innovation. This discovery is supported in other disciplines. For example, scholars analyzed years of biomedical research collaborations in one American city and found an indirect relationship between the physical distance separating the offices of the key research partners and the importance of the papers. In other words, the shorter the distance, the more likely the paper was to be highly influential.[71] Based on outcomes such as these, some researchers have pulled up roots and moved their offices closer to their collaborators—despite all the possibilities for communication now offered through the Internet. Proximity is an organizational strategy to spark innovative thinking.

Some universities, such as the Massachusetts Institute of Technology, have actively promoted proximity by clustering the labs of inventive scientists in ideas centers.[72] Japanese schools are similarly structured so that teachers have time to meet together outside the classroom. There is an assumption that teachers can be the source of solutions for the problems of education. There is nothing in the research that signals that the best ideas are coming from the top leaders in the field. Rather, the ideas are signaling where the leadership lies.

## REORGANIZATION

Reorganization is a common leadership tactic that can stimulate new ways of thinking. One leader explained,

> One of the surest ways to get a job done more innovatively is, quite simply, to reorganize frequently. When you put people into a new structure, it stimulates them to rethink what they're doing on a day-to-day basis. . . . We needed to orient people toward a new goal, and reorganizing was one way to do that.[73]

Reorganization abruptly changes the organizational culture and signals that the status quo is not acceptable. When fundamental change is required and long-standing beliefs and practices cannot be tolerated, then reorganization can be effective. This is the thinking behind some of the school turnaround strategies, where whole schools can be reconstituted or one school dissolved and an entirely new school created in its stead.

Reorganization, however, is a blunt tool. The tactic definitely signals the end of old ways but cannot predict what will replace it. This is not a sure route to an institutional practice of adaptive learning. In fact, Kanter was critical of the crude shuffling of assets in large organizations such as urban school districts. She wrote,

> The view of a corporation as merely a bundle of movable assets (a "portfolio") turns attention away from long-term productivity and innovation, both of which require internal investment. Faced with increasing uncertainties and with "political" tasks in a politicized environment, chief executives sometimes find it easier to imagine shedding what is *not* working and acquiring what *is* working elsewhere than to undertake the longer, more tedious, more difficult, and less glamorous task of reorienting—changing—their own core company.[74]

Many American districts now employ a portfolio approach, which presents a smorgasbord of specialized schools that can differ by size, academic theme, special services, technology, curriculum, schedules, or even governance. Increasingly, charter schools are part of that mix. Choice may be a good way to personalize services for children and to increase parental engagement, but choice alone is not a substitute for critical self-analysis and adaptive learning.

Too often, choice can distract from central office problems. Old, underperforming schools are shuttered, while new ones are developed, which gives the appearance of bold leadership. For students and families who develop local school loyalties, however, the process of changing schools is disruptive and perilous.

At the core of successful schools of every size and type are competent teachers and leaders who engage in an ongoing process of experimentation and innovation to best meet the changing needs of students. Staffing, therefore, is a preeminent concern. In some districts, the "shopping-around-for-solutions" philosophy can prevail in staffing, too. There are many promising alternative routes to teaching and school leadership today, such as Teach for America and New Leaders. In the end, however, every teacher and leader has to learn entrepreneurial skills, such as how to identify problems, experiment with new solutions, spot momentary opportunities, and take an idea to implementation.

In the 1980s students were offered a smorgasbord of curricular choices because there were no academic standards. The practice was soundly criticized in a book called *The Shopping Mall High School*.[75] Today, the same shopping mall approach can be suspected when a district develops a portfolio of schools or looks for new outlets for teachers and leaders. Is frantic shopping a sign of creative experimentation and innovation or just a distraction from larger systemic problems?

The focus of this chapter is on institutional constraints that curb entrepreneurial leadership. Frederick Hess, a well-known writer on educational reform wrote, "I contend that the rarely addressed issue of institutional constraints ought to be a topic of keen interest to educators and policymakers, and that the pedagogical and leadership practices that receive so much attention ought to be issues of lesser concern."[76] Thankfully, there has been far more interest in the organizational culture of districts in recent years.[77] More and more, scholars are willing to say, "If you have ineffective schools, that is a district problem, not a school problem."[78]

## INCENTIVES

Another possible way to stimulate entrepreneurial leadership is through the use of incentives. One national figure claimed,

> Policymakers who wish to unleash more entrepreneurial energy in struggling school systems should consider an approach that makes risk taking more glamorous and rewarding than is currently the case. Pay scales for teachers and principals currently leave little room for incentives that reward risk taking to find better ways to educate children.[79]

While the call for entrepreneurial energy is commendable, resorting to pay scales is misguided. Given the independent determination found in entrepreneurs, incentivizing innovation with pay bumps may be futile. In fact, there is often a disparity between what human resource managers believe would motivate intrapreneurs and what really in fact works.[80]

Canadian researcher Camille Carrier also studied motivation for intrapreneurship in small businesses; many of the firms were themselves started by entrepreneurs.[81] In this portion of her study, she was looking at the *personal* motivators for intrapreneurs, independent of organizational characteristics.

In keeping with Herzberg's two-factor theory,[82] Carrier found both intrinsic and extrinsic factors. According to Herzberg, intrinsic factors can increase personal motivation, while extrinsic factors can explain the loss of job satisfaction when they are absent, but do little to boost motivation. For example, while outdated equipment or a broken copy machine can lead to a loss of job satisfaction, their replacement does little to motivate teachers to improve their practice. At the same time, teachers are motivated by the intrinsic reward of love for children or the magic of "seeing the light go on" in a learner's eyes. Research demonstrates that pay scales and incidental stipends are extrinsic factors that affect job satisfaction, but do little to affect motivation.

Carrier found that the intrinsic motivators for intrapreneurs included the challenge itself, the love of learning-rich work, the sense of working for oneself, controlling one's destiny, and a love for efficiency. Similar to teachers, the extrinsic factors for intrapreneurs, which affected job satisfaction, included recognition, promotion, bonuses, and salary.

Similarly, in large firms, researchers have found that promotion (which means power and pay increases) is not the motivation for intrapreneurship.[83] More than a pay bump, intrapreneurs want the freedom to innovate—with all that implies in terms of time for imagining, experimentation, risk-taking, and failure—as well as resources specific to their projects. In other words, money to support the development of an innovation is more likely to motivate an entrepreneur than a stipend in the paycheck. In small firms, entrepreneurs did want promotion—but primarily to get closer to the owner-manager, who would then give them greater freedom and resources to carry out their projects.

What does this mean for the promotion of entrepreneurism in the teaching profession? Many people have called for increased time for collaboration among teachers, but they interpret the common obstacles in one of two ways. Some would like teachers to work longer days so they can collaborate, but they criticize the unions when teachers demand compensation. Others see the need to pay teachers for added time but point to budgets already stretched too thin. Both interpretations, however, view teachers through the narrow lens of piecemeal employees while ignoring Herzberg's two-factor theory of motivation.

In truth, teachers volunteer to work all the time, proving that they are motivated by other factors. They devote uncounted hours to correcting homework, creating new curricular units, tutoring students, and summer enrichment projects—but always on their terms, voluntarily. Obviously, entrepreneurs want to do their own thing. They want administrators to get out of their way, and while they are not so motivated by a stipend, they do hope for support instead of impediments. Instead of compensation, what is needed is a wider consideration of the things that really motivate teachers. Money is nice, but teachers do not join up just to make a lot of money.

There are two other ways to think about incentives. The first approach looks to the innovative educator, with respect to the things that motivate entrepreneurs. When Kanter studied large corporations in the 1980s, she found the reward systems in non-entrepreneurial companies were retroactive; in other words, they paid people for their accomplishments. However, "the innovative companies 'invested' in people before they carried out their projects."[84] The reward to the intrapreneur was getting the opportunity to pursue the innovation, with the promise of company support as it began to emerge. These companies were investment oriented, rather than payoff oriented, and promotions were not a reward for doing the last job but a bet on capacity for doing the next one. This is a fresh way of thinking about unleashing entrepreneurism in teachers.

The second approach recognizes that there are many innovations in education, but not all benefit the family customers. When writing about organizational characteristics that predicted intrapreneurship, Hentschke and Caldwell contrasted the "cost centre" model and the "revenue centre" model of funding.[85] In the former, the leader used a budget line to support inventiveness, but the institutional focus on cost containment distracted from customer satisfaction. On the other hand, the revenue center model began with a focus on consumer satisfaction, which was a constant propellant to doing things better.

Hess made this point when he wrote, "Schooling must move decisively away from a system governed by inputs and regulation to one ordered around individuals and results."[86] The cost center model focused on leader satisfaction, while the latter focused on customer satisfaction and was more likely to produce truly effective innovations. Too many school districts have been run by short-term superintendents whose precipitous innovations are sure to build their résumé and please the school committee, but are not necessarily in the best interests of children in the long run.[87]

On the other hand, one would predict that a focus on student and family outcomes would lead to a pattern of experimentation with tentative steps, ongoing measurement, and a legacy of practical, substantive innovations. There certainly is a public dissatisfaction with the status quo and a demand for innovation. The long waiting lists for certain charter schools, where innovations such as a longer school day and year, the use of technology, advisories, and portfolio exhibitions are popular, support this argument. Many question whether charter schools are the answer to America's educational system, but they are perceived as a welcome source of experimentation.

## THE EARLY COLLEGE CASE STUDY RECONSIDERED

Chapter 2 told the story of an early college program, which helped academically average high school students earn college credits and increased their readiness for post-secondary education. This was a case of growing entrepreneurial leadership from an opportunistic to a more frame-breaking level. What were the organizational conditions that facilitated this kind of leadership?

One obvious advantage was that the district was small, with a hierarchy that was flat compared to some large urban districts. The principal and superintendent talked together every day. The guidance counselor, who first identified the idea, had easy access to the principal. Pulling a team together for bimonthly meetings was relatively simple.

The high school had a well-developed partnership with the local community college. As a result, the guidance counselor knew just who to call to discuss her idea. The two institutions were used to negotiating budgets, schedules, and staffing. There was a high level of trust. The benefit of partnerships, such as this one, cannot be overstated and will be taken up again in chapter 6.

Creative people are motivated intrinsically by the challenge, the joy of creating, and personal interest. The guidance counselor enjoyed creating new services for students who did not do well in high school or college. This principal recalled his own struggles as young teenager without direction and the power that high expectations had on his life. They were engaged by the challenge of cutting through the interorganizational red tape and doing something unprecedented. They also had time in their schedules, literally giving hundreds of hours over several years to develop the project. Creative thinkers need time.

In this case, the guidance counselor was the *idea champion*, who regularly advocated for her struggling students. She found a *sponsor* in the community college dean, who became an indispensable ally. The principal and, later, the superintendent played a *godfather* role, making sure the idea gained traction and was not dismissed or destroyed by skeptics. Together, they met bimonthly as a planning team, which became the *greenhouse* for the early college concept. Here, they plotted strategy, such as when to bring in key stakeholders and how to address union and accreditation issues. As a result, the early college program was able to take root.

The high school was loosely structured, like most schools, despite efforts to the contrary. The early college program was somewhat isolated from the rest of the school, which facilitated experimentation and innovation at the classroom level. This was a daily event, since the instructors were still feeling their way with a co-teaching model and an integrated curriculum. Employees in the rest of the school knew about the program, but there was very little exchange of information or practices.

The *greenhouse* effect can protect the pilot project but also prevent publication and dissemination so the innovation is never replicated. In this case, the planning team decided to record and evaluate everything and publish the results. As a result, as the early outcomes were promising, the partners began to duplicate the program in other schools.

Social learning theory offers light on the organizational components of success. At least three members of the planning team exhibited entrepreneurial traits, which they modeled proudly to the rest of the team and outside stakeholders. When other members were less tolerant of risk or raised objections, the entrepreneurial trio was quick to offer solutions and moral persuasion that highlighted the achievement gap.

They provided resources. In some ways, this was the most extraordinary aspect of the entrepreneurism. For months, the college, high school, and district leaders hammered out the details of curriculum, scheduling, and staffing with little discussion of expenses. When they finally put a memorandum of agreement on the table, the figures were still tentative. The college and the district entered into the agreement with fuzzy estimates of the real costs. Furthermore, rather than challenging the cost with each ensuing year, the district and college leaders insisted that they had to run the full five-year experiment to make a true cost-benefit analysis.

The leaders demonstrated enabling behaviors. Cheerleading was obvious, especially when the first families began to sign up and students succeeded academically. The top leaders often recognized and praised the intrapreneurs. The principal, for example, repeatedly reminded participants that the early college program would not work in any high school without a guidance counselor with the same talent and determination as they enjoyed. The leaders showed their recognition and appreciation when they took their innovative staff to regional and national conferences.

The K–12 district and college both had somewhat traditional, segmentalist structures where territoriality was always a threat. Faculty departments worried about the curriculum in the early college classes, the institutional unions worried about violations of the contractual agreements, and financial officers worried about unintended costs. In this respect, the two institutions, separately, were not models of integrative cultures.

The planning team worked strategically to bring important stakeholders onto the team or into the conversation, while avoiding the mistake of broadcasting every innovative idea, which would open them to unnecessary criticism. As they brought various departments together across two institutions, the culture became more deliberately integrative. For example, the community college now has a director of strategic initiatives whose mission is work across departments to multiple similar high school–college partnerships.

After several years, the organizational structure around the early college program became clearer. The planning team was still meeting in the fifth year of the program. This team, which included high school administrators and guidance counselors as well as several mid-level college administrators, had a matrix-like organizational quality. They met voluntarily, they met as equals, and they all participated and communicated both inside and outside the meetings. At the same time, the classrooms were not a matrix. Although the instructors practiced student-centered pedagogies, there was no question of who was in charge.

In the fourth year, the district superintendent ceased attending the planning meetings, as did the college vice president of academics. Increasingly, top management wanted a paper-and-pencil analysis of costs and benefits. After a few rounds of replication, the community college began to look for ways to standardize the college readiness programs. They appointed a new administrator to oversee the work who began to raise questions about faculty schedules, classroom rigor, and student transcripts. To the veteran team members, this did not feel like a matrix.

To summarize, the early college program grew up to fulfill Kanter's prediction. The mid-level planning team continued to operate with a matrix-like organizational structure, which allowed for innovation. The top layers of both organizations returned to a focus on accountability and reminded the team of state laws, academic standards, and accreditation, while the students at the bottom layer, in the classrooms, received the innovations of the planning team.

Furthermore, the early college program rejected a cost-centered model of funding in favor of a revenue-centered model. For two years, the leaders on the planning team tried to ignore costs while building the program they believed would work for children and families. This approach was conducive to innovative thinking, for the budgetary threat was removed from the table. At the end of two years, they welcomed the first cohort of students even as they drew up a tentative memorandum of agreement that specified costs between the two educational institutions and the parents.

Kanter discovered that innovative companies invested in their entrepreneurs in advance, rather than compensating them afterward for success. The early college program took this same approach. The leaders singled out teachers they believed were entrepreneurial—teachers who were bold, experimentally minded, excited by challenges, and not afraid of hard work. They paid the teachers for two weeks of summer planning. And they gave them a blank slate to create the new early college curriculum.

There were no extrinsic motivators in the early college program beyond the stipends for the summer professional development. These two weeks gave faculty members from the college and high school an opportunity to meet one another and begin writing an integrated curriculum for a course they would co-teach. During the year, however, the high school instructors received their normal compensation and the college faculty was paid by the same hourly rate even though the work was extreme.

The program presented many new challenges. Instructors had to create new lesson plans and learn a co-teaching pedagogy. There was a significant cultural challenge as the high school teachers grappled with college expectations and college faculty learned to accommodate immature students. Due to the fact that the program recruited underachieving students and exposed them to the rigors of college coursework, the teachers found they had to provide extraordinary levels of support. This required far more time for after-school tutoring and communication with parents.

Why would teachers volunteer for all this added work? Amabile's work on creativity has direct application here. Like many innovative people, these teachers loved what they were doing. The challenge of the work, the experimentation, the exploration of something new, and the joy of seeing students succeed were all intrinsic motivators that more than compensated the teachers. Creative work is fun. Public education offers far too few opportunities for creative work, especially as curriculum standards, pacing guides, and standardized achievement tests dominate the field.

The teachers loved the liberty to create. More than once, they expressed the joy of being released from school-wide curricular standards. For example, the high school required most English teachers to employ "focused essays," where writing was scaffolded and students were graded on only two or three writing points at a time. However, the early college English teacher was co-teaching a college-level class. She gloated,

> I can get away without scaffolding my work because I work with college professors. . . . I don't have to teach with focused essays because the college professors are creating the same set of essays and they don't know what the hell they are![88]

## CONCLUSION

Entrepreneurialism is not just an individual talent but often a team effort. Innovative people need freedom to imagine and experiment, encouragement to persevere through setbacks, and support in terms of materials and information. While they say they "just want to be left alone," in reality, they are dependent on their social networks for new ideas and resources. Increasingly, entrepreneurialism is understood to be an organizational phenomenon more than an individual accomplishment.

The early college program encouraged frame-breaking innovation through organizational structures that proved to be entrepreneur-friendly. While separately, the high school and the community college were segmentalist cultures, together they created a partnership with an integrative culture. Two of the top leaders were accomplished business entrepreneurs, so they appreciated the conditions that encouraged creative thinking and they were wary of the impediments to innovation. However, the principles that guided their decisions were not always explicit.

This chapter analyzed the organizational characteristics that help or hinder intrapreneurs. Many of these lessons came from business books that are thirty years old, for entrepreneurial leadership was appreciated and studied more intensively in that field. This speaks to the relative conservatism of public education and highlights the need for fresh thinking.

Educational institutions can learn to be integrative, entrepreneurial cultures. The pressures of international competition combined with the changing demographic nature of the American student population demand new approaches in education. Too often, educators double down on accountability schemes, which yield marginal gains, while extinguishing creativity. The early college program broke out of this framework and produced measurable gains for underachieving students. While students enjoyed the challenge and re-enrolled year after year, their parents were saving money on the cost of college, and the teachers were re-experiencing the satisfaction of creating new solutions and watching students succeed.

## NOTES

1. Craig Wynett of Procter & Gamble; Inspiring innovation. (2002). *Harvard Business Review, 80*(8), 40.

2. Kanter, R. M. (1983). *The change masters: Innovation and entrepreneurship in the American corporation.* New York: Simon & Schuster, Inc.

3. Kanter, R. M., 132.

4. Lavaroni, C. W., & Leisey, D. E. The edupreneur: Bringing the excitement of entrepreneurism to the public schools. Retrieved May 8, 2010, from http://www.edentrepreneurs.org/edupreneur.phtm.

5. Kay, K. (2011, November 9). Unleashing locally driven innovation. *Education Week, 31,* 32.

6. Williams, J. (2006). Breaking the mold: How do school entrepreneurs create change? *Education Next, 6*(2), 45.

7. Carrier, C. (1996). Intrapreneurship in small businesses: An exploratory study. *Entrepreneurship: Theory & Practice, 21*(1), 5–20; Kanter, R. M.; Pinchot, G., III. (1985). *Intrapreneuring: Why you don't have to leave the corporation to become an entrepreneur.* New York: Harper & Row.

8. Kouzes and Posner wrote a highly acclaimed book on leadership and noted that "leaders aren't the only creators or originators of new products, services, or processes. In fact, it's more likely that they're not; innovation

comes more from listening than from telling." Kouzes, J. M., & Posner, B. Z. (2008). *The leadership challenge* (4th ed., p. 19). San Francisco: Jossey-Bass.

9. Kouzes, J. M., & Posner, B. Z., 19.

10. These rules are compiled from the following two sources: Kanter, R. M. (1983), 101; Kanter, R. M. (2013, January 15). Nine rules for stifling innovation. Retrieved from http://blogs.hbr.org/kanter/2013/01/nine-rules-for-stifling-innova.html.

11. Kanter, R. M. (1983), 101.

12. Kanter, R. M. (1983), 101.

13. Kanter, R. M. (2013), para. 4.

14. Kanter, R. M. (2013), para. 5.

15. Kanter, R. M. (2013), para. 6.

16. Kanter, R. M. (1983), 101.

17. Kanter, R. M. (2013), para. 9.

18. Kanter, R. M. (1983), 101.

19. Kanter, R. M. (1983), 101.

20. Kanter, R. M. (2013), para. 8.

21. Kanter, R. M. (1983), p. 101.

22. Kanter, R. M. (2013), para. 11.

23. Kanter, R. M. (1983).

24. Adams, K. (2005). *The sources of innovation and creativity* (p. 59). Washington, DC: National Center on Education and the Economy; Amabile, T. M. (1997). Motivating creativity in organizations: On doing what you love and loving what you do. *California Management Review, 40*(1), 39–58; Amabile, T. M. (1998). How to kill creativity. *Harvard Business Review, 76*(5), 76–87.

25. Adams, K.

26. Adams, K.

27. Vitagliano, R., & Khan, S. (2007). *Teacher as social entrepreneur: Practices of an innovative and resourceful urban elementary school teacher.* Paper presented at the annual meeting of the American Educational Research Association, Chicago, IL.

28. Kanter, R. M. (1983).

29. Kolderie, T. (2011, November 8). A "split-screen strategy" for innovation. *Education Week, 31,* 24–25.

30. Scott was cited in Werter, L. Y. (2011). *Has someone seen my spark? Entrepreneurship in Oxfam Novib.* Master's degree thesis, Universiteit Utrecht, Utrecht. Retrieved from http://igitur-archive.library.uu.nl/student-theses/2011-1118-200806/UUindex.html.

31. Kanter, R. M. (1983).

32. Tung, R., Ouimette, M., & Rugen, L. (2006). Progress and promise: Results from the Boston pilot schools. Boston, MA: Center for Collaborative Education.

33. Inspiring innovation. (2002). *Harvard Business Review, 80*(8), 39–49.

34. Dubin, A. E. (1991). *The principal as chief executive officer* (p. 11). Bristol, PA: Falmer Press.

35. Carrier, C.

36. Carrier, C., 11.

37. Snyder, K. J., & Anderson, R. H. (1987). What principals can learn from corporate management. *Principal, 66*(4), 22–26.

38. Snyder, K. J., & Anderson, R. H., 26.

39. Snyder, K. J., & Anderson, R. H., 26.

40. Kay, K.

41. Bandura, A. (1997). *Self-Efficacy: The exercise of control.* New York: W. H. Freeman and Company.

42. Kanter, R. M. (2013).

43. Carrier, C., 11.

44. Snyder, K. J., & Anderson, R. H., 26, quoting Pinchot, G., III., 315.

45. Eyal, O., & Kark, R. (2004). How do transformational leaders transform organizations? A study of the relationship between leadership and entrepreneurship. *Leadership and Policy in Schools, 3*(3), 212.

46. Carrier, C.

47. Kanter, R. M. (1983), 27.

48. Kanter, R. M. (1983), 114.

49. Kanter, R. M. (1983), 55.

50. Kanter, R. M. (1983), 134.

51. Kanter, R. M. (1983), 136.

52. Eyal, O., & Kark, R., 229 (italics added).

53. Weick, K. E. (1982). Management of organizational change among loosely coupled elements. In P. S. Goodman & Associates (Eds.), *Change in Organizations* (pp. 375–408). Washington: Jossey-Bass; Weick, K. E. (1983). Educational organizations as loosely coupled systems. In J. V. Baldridge & T. E. Deal (Eds.), *The dynamics of organizational change in education* (pp. 15–37). Berkeley, CA: McCutchan Publishing Corporation.

54. Weick, K. E. (1982).

55. Weick, K. E. (1982).

56. Weick, K. E. (1982), 387.

57. Weick, K. E. (1982).

58. Kanter, R. M. (1983).

59. Kanter, R. M. (1983), 146.

60. Louis, K. S., & Miles, M. B. (1990). *Improving the urban high school: What works and why.* New York: Teachers College Press.

61. Kanter, R. M. (1983), 146; this organizational structure is further developed in chapters 4 and 5.

62. Kanter, R. M. (1983), 147.

63. Hill, P. T. (2003). Entrepreneurship in K–12 public education. In M. L. Kourilsky & W. B. Walstad (Eds.), *Social Entrepreneurship* (p. 65): Senate Hall Academic Publishing.

64. Kanter, R. M. (1983), 147.

65. Kanter, R. M. (1983), 147.

66. DuFour, R., & Eaker, R. (1998). *Professional learning communities at work: Best practices for enhancing student achievement.* Bloomington, IN: Solution Tree.

67. Heifetz, R. A., & Linsky, M. (2002). *Leadership on the line: Staying alive through the dangers of leading.* Boston: Harvard Business School Press.

68. Ouchi, W. G. (1982). *Theory Z.* New York: Avon Publishers.

69. Snyder, K. J., & Anderson, R. H., 24–25, citing Deal & Kennedy, *Corporate Cultures* (1982).

70. Metropolitan Life Insurance (2010). *The MetLife survey of the American teacher: Collaborating for student success.* Metropolitan Life Insurance Company.

71. Johnson, C. Y. (2011, May 8). Collaboration: the mother of invention. *The Boston Globe,* p. B1. Retrieved from http://www.boston.com/news/science/articles/2011/05/08/for_researchers_in_boston_area_close_quarters_help_elevate_their_work/.

72. MIT Media Lab. (2011). Retrieved December 1, 2011, from http://www.media.mit.edu/

73. Inspiring innovation, 41.

74. Kanter, R. M. (1983), 51.

75. Powell, A. G., Farrar, E., & Cohen, D. K. (1985). *The shopping mall high school: Winners and losers in the educational marketplace.* Boston: Houghton Mifflin Company.

76. Hess, F. M. (1999). *Spinning wheels: The politics of urban school reform* (p. 17). Washington, DC: Brookings Institution Press.

77. Honig, M. I., Copland, M. A., Rainey, L., Lorton, J. A., & Newton, M. (2010). *Central office transformation for district-wide teaching and learning improvement.* Center for the Study of Teaching and Policy; Orr, M. T., King, C., & LaPointe, M. (2010). *Districts developing leaders: Lessons on consumer actions and program approaches from eight urban districts* (p. 152). Newton, MA: Education Development Center.

78. Annual convention of the University Council for Educational Administration. (2011). Personal communication.

79. Williams, J., 49.

80. Marvel, M. R., Griffin, A., Hebda, J., & Vojak, B. (2007). Examining the technical corporate entrepreneurs' motivation: Voices from the field. *Entrepreneurship: Theory & Practice, 31*(5), 753–768.

81. Carrier, C.

82. Herzberg, F. (1973). *Work and the nature of man.* New York: Mentor Book.

83. Carrier, C.; Kanter, R. M. (1983).

84. Kanter, R. M. (1983), 154.

85. Hentschke, G., & Caldwell, B. J. (2005). Entrepreneurial leadership. In B. Davies (Ed.), *The essentials of school leadership* (p. 156). Thousand Oaks, CA: Corwin Press.

86.  Hess, F. M. (2007). *Reimagining American schooling: The case for educational entrepreneurship* (vol. 4, para. 29). Washington, DC: American Enterprise Institute for Public Policy Research.

87.  Hess, F. M. (1999).

88.  Leonard, J. (2013). Cross-cultural communities of practice for college readiness (p. 13). Manuscript submitted for publication.

# 4

# LEADING AN ENTREPRENEURIAL ORGANIZATION

**E**ntrepreneurial leaders are a unique breed, not always charismatic, sometimes transformational, but always open to new ideas that might solve tough problems. Importantly, most entrepreneurs do not emerge at the top of their organization, but from the ranks. The position of leadership does not breed entrepreneurial thinking; rather, entrepreneurial thinking promotes people toward a leadership role. In light of the relentless demand for innovation in education, what is needed is not just a one-shot entrepreneur but an entrepreneurial leader who can lead an innovative learning organization.

This chapter uses a historical case study to develop an argument for entrepreneurial leadership. The case study uncovers the sources of innovation and helps clarify the role of the leader in a learning organization. For educational reform work, a cultural reform strategy is contrasted with traditional structural and curricular reform models. The challenge of scalability is addressed head-on. The chapter ends with an urgent appeal for moral leadership.

The stories here are written for principals, irrespective of grade level and regardless of whether they head up traditional K–12 schools, alternative, charter, private, pilot, or magnet schools; career academies; or any other variation. Superintendents or school committee members might appreciate this chapter to think about the selection of better school leaders.

This chapter will be a let-down for some leaders, for it steers clear of the hard-charging, charismatic leader and introduces a much less exciting version. The focus of this chapter is the leader for the entrepreneurial organization, an exciting and inspiring place to work where the top CEO might not be the all-star.

Here is a common scenario in public schools. The leader has the ego-presence to be the chief executive but the humility to know that he or she is not entirely in charge. One principal might joke that his secretary makes all the important decisions while another shares the credit with his management team. There is a self-conscious uneasiness about this truth, combined with the determination to remain at the top. No wonder school leaders often fall into the trap of providing technical solutions that fall short in the face of adaptive challenges.

This chapter contains a number of confessions. Unlike the rest of the book, which relies on anecdotes from around the world, much of the information in this chapter is taken from the history of the Boston school where I served and my experience there as a school teacher, mid-level administrator, and high school headmaster. For that reason, the voice and tone of the chapter is often different.

## A CASE STUDY: DUNBAR HIGH

Dunbar High School (DHS) was founded in 1852, expanded into different buildings as the city grew up around it, and came to rest in a classical building on Dunbar Street in 1925. At one time, the school was an all-boys vocational school, but girls were added in the 1950s. By the 1960s, the school was one of the better schools in the city with an admirable record of serving Irish and Italian immigrants alongside the Jewish families who lived in the neighborhood. Notably, the school also welcomed the new Black families that were slowly moving into the neighborhood.[1]

Over the next forty years, however, the school followed a roller-coaster ride of ups and downs. The public perception was one of racial strife and violence, even as the school was inventing new models of personalization that would spread to other schools. At one point, the school chalked up the highest dropout rate in the state and then, just a few years later, was gaining national attention for radical structural reforms. The history of the last forty years was amply documented, offering a close-up view of events.[2]

The racial strife, which made this city famous, did not leave Dunbar untouched. The golden years of the 1960s were followed by horrific strife in the 1970s as this school changed overnight from a white immigrant school to a warehouse for low-income Black students. Two thousand students were assigned to this old building, which had a capacity for one thousand seats. Teaching was doubly complicated by new federal and state laws, which mandated special services to students with disabilities and English language learners.

There were two bright spots in the subsequent history of the school. In the 1980s the school experienced a relief in student assignments and a kind of cultural renaissance, which was evident with improved freshmen retention rates, climbing school attendance rates, and a much safer school culture.[3] Then, with the economic recession of 1988–1992, the school sank into despair again. Newspaper articles documented the violence, including several deaths, so that by 1993 Dunbar had the highest dropout rate of any comprehensive high school in the state. In 1996 their accreditation was threatened when the regional accrediting agency put the school on probation.

In yet another reversal, by 2000 the school was fully accredited, student metrics were again improving, and the school won coveted recognition from a local foundation. Inquiring visitors came from all over the country to learn how the school had restructured into small learning communities for freshmen, non-traditional learners, and other students interested in business, technology, and public service. Conditions for students continued to improve in the following decade.

These two bright spots in Dunbar's history—the mid-1980s and the twelve years from 1997 to 2008—showed some common patterns. Both periods were marked by startling, creative, energetic innovation. Again, the lesson of chapter 1 bears repeating: as long as available evidence indicates that what we are doing is not meeting the needs of students, there will always be a need for innovation. Both periods are instructive.

## INNOVATION IN THE 1980s

School reform at Dunbar High began with outside pressures calling for better student outcomes. In 1983 the National Commission on Excellence in Education published *A Nation at Risk*, bringing the alarming message that "our once unchallenged preeminence in commerce, industry, science, and technological innovation is being overtaken by competitors throughout the world" who are better educated and more motivated.[4]

At the same time, in Boston, a consortium of downtown businesses called the Private Industry Council (PIC) signed an agreement with the school superintendent and the city's mayor, which promised jobs for high school graduates if the city could increase student achievement and graduation rates. This revolutionary agreement, called the Boston

Compact, was backed up with money, which came from state grants as well as a new city educational foundation financed by the PIC.

The Boston Compact provided motivation and money for school change. This was one of the first examples in the nation of city-scale partnerships to address the intransigent problems of public education.[5] Under the Compact, every school was mandated to engage, but the shape of school change could be locally determined. Scholars call this an evolutionary planning strategy.[6] In contrast to the goal-based accountability strategy (see chapter 3), where the district specified the achievement goals and left the process up to the local school, in this case, the district dictated the broad structure for reform, but left the achievement goals in the hands of the local school. Both strategies involved a coordination of district-level and school-based reform efforts.

Two researchers who followed school reform at Dunbar in this time period called the Compact "a partially filled vessel into which locally developed school plans were to be poured."[7] This outside pressure to "fix things," combined with the freedom to decide internally how best to use the new resources, proved instrumental for entrepreneurial creativity at DHS.

The second lesson from the 1980s reform was the importance of community partnerships. The Boston Compact, which sparked reform, was a citywide partnership between the PIC and the Boston Public Schools. Dunbar also enjoyed local community partners in the New England Telephone Company and the University of Massachusetts Boston. These institutions began working with the school in the 1970s. In the 1980s they teamed up with the school again to plan and implement change.

Success at Dunbar came through small-scale (*bricoleur*) innovations, which were spearheaded by creative and motivated staff members who were empowered by the Boston Compact, the evolutionary planning strategy, and the community partnerships. The most significant innovations took the form of small learning communities, which personalized services to students. In Boston in the 1980s, when "white flight" was gutting school enrollments, magnet school programs were a popular remedy.

Some small learning communities at Dunbar had magnet themes, such as health, public service, and the law. Others targeted specific student populations. For example, one small community called the LAB Cluster was created to serve students with moderate emotional and behavioral disabilities. This model was perfected at Dunbar and later replicated across the state. Therefore, this *bricoleur* innovation grew to the stage of social constructivism.

A second small learning community, which was created with a particular group of students in mind and funded by the Boston Compact, was a freshmen academy called Compact Ventures. New England Telephone and UMass Boston were directly involved in this creation, which focused on ninth graders who were at risk of dropping out. The community partners bolstered the school leadership. New England Telephone offered leadership seminars for teachers and department chairs. They also offered guest speakers for the ninth grade classrooms. Both partners consulted privately with the headmaster and were able to address predictable gaps in experience, such as working with the media. As a result, Compact Ventures was well publicized and favorably reviewed by the *Boston Globe* for over five years.

Everyone knew that dropout rates peaked in the ninth grade in the city high schools. Pregnancy rates were so high that Dunbar started a parenting class in 1983. The average daily attendance for freshmen at the beginning of this program was only 80 percent.

The academy was built on innovative practices. The academy had a dedicated director, who only focused on 110 at-risk students. There was a youth worker who engaged with truant students and their families. Class sizes were reduced with teaching assistants. The teachers, assistants, and counselors met daily in common planning-time sessions to coordinate their efforts. The community partners provided motivational speakers as well as individual prizes and classroom plaques for improved attendance. There were also after-school activities.

Irene Sege of the *Boston Globe* chronicled the early outcomes:

> When fifty of the poorest readers were tested in September they were reading like early fifth graders. By June, their average score was mid-year seventh grade, a jump of more than two years. . . . Median scores on standardized math and reading tests were up. In a special program designed to give extra support services for about half the school's ninth graders, twelve students—11 percent—dropped out. The schoolwide freshman dropout rate was 22 percent last year.[8]

As a result, Compact Ventures was expanded to the entire ninth grade the following year and, later, to the tenth grade. The Compact Ventures initiative sparked a school-wide change in culture that brought school pride back to Dunbar in 1985. There were gains on the new citywide student achievement tests, which was encouraging news after the previous year when DHS had posted the worst high school test scores in the district.

The two researchers who followed this process could conclude:

As of 1986, the prospects at Dunbar appeared bright: The strategy was in place, a cohesive management team was emerging, staff skepticism and resistance were diminishing among most groups, and there was plenty of help to design support and assistance strategies. The trajectory was toward real improvement. Several program aspects seemed well routinized (central administrative planning, job development, and work on discipline and climate), but others less so (the departmental planning, curriculum development, and supervision aspects).[9]

These were innovations in that they were *new to the school*, but not necessarily unprecedented in education. This is an important point. Pablo Picasso, one of the world's most innovative artists, admitted, "Good artists copy, great artists steal." One business scholar went on to say, "Innovators sometimes make the mistake of assuming they get extra points for doing something difficult, or something that's never been done before. But remember, innovation is something different *that has impact.*"[10] For the leaders, teachers, partners, parents, and students of Compact Ventures in the mid-1980s, there was a sense of movement. This was new. They were experimenting and trying out new approaches, rather than surrendering to the "same-old, same-old." They were addressing real problems with concrete solutions. The sense of promise in itself was motivating.

In the 1980s freshmen academies like Compact Ventures were an entrepreneurial innovation. This was a local idea, which was later replicated across the city and hailed by the media and the state department of education. Like the LAB Cluster, the freshmen academy for at-risk youth grew to become a social constructivist project.

Boston published an annual compendium of school data called *School Profiles*; Dunbar High's page in the 1985 edition boasted with pride:

> Major Accomplishments: Improved academic performance Read/ Math tests, cited by Massachusetts Board of Education as effective urban school, recognized by governor for implementing alternative programs, attendance improved, ninth grade dropout rate reduced by 50 percent, received *Boston Globe* Nason Award for athletic excellence, PIC Program placed 160 students in summer full-time jobs, New England Telephone hired students, 50 percent of college course students were placed, over 50 percent of parents attended a school event, eighteen organizations provide direct services to students and staff. Special programs are Urban Scholars, Student Challenge, Army Junior ROTC, Health Careers, Home Improvement Enterprise, Compact Ventures, Student Support Team, comprehensive adolescent parenting program.[11]

In this case study, outside pressures combined with internal entrepreneurial imagination and the support of community partners sparked a flurry of innovation. As chapter 3 predicted, the organizational structures were loose enough to allow local innovation and adaptability. The community partnerships helped address the resource needs but declined to dictate the shape of the innovations. The delivery mechanisms that brought students to the point where they could read and write and graduate were created locally, inside the school. The overall organizational culture was conducive to entrepreneurism.

Compact Ventures was replicated in eight other high schools. However, by 1989 the national economic recession undercut state and local support so, predictably, the program died.

## SCALABILITY

Some will criticize the Compact Ventures initiative as not sustainable or scalable. I'm sure the Dunbar ninth graders who found success that year were not complaining, but others have bemoaned the fact that while public education is flooded with innovations, few are scalable.[12] Critics point to local, idiosyncratic accommodating policies, targeted grant support (such as the Boston Compact), unusual staff expertise, or fleeting enthusiasm that breed local innovation but limit large-scale replication.[13] Some question whether large-scale change is even possible in the entrenched institutional culture of most public school systems and suggest that new, for-profit organizations would be a better source for scalable educational innovations. This line of thinking departs from the purpose of this book, which argues for entrepreneurial innovation inside the schoolhouse.

There are two ways to think about educational innovation. One is to identify a few scalable innovations and duplicate them everywhere. The problem with this approach is that the scalable innovations are few in number. Furthermore, this approach can lead to heavy-handed innovations that stymie local input. For example, teachers often complain about "teacher-proof" curricular units that are guaranteed to work but insult the professional expertise of the teacher. When a competent English teacher is mandated to replicate a certain curriculum and pedagogy faithfully, there is less opportunity to craft strategies, day by day, that might address the obvious needs in the classroom. Experimentation, risk-taking, and discovery are actually discouraged.

The fixation on scalability might actually discourage creative innovation on the ground. The very conditions that critics disparage—local, accommodating policies, targeted grant support, unusual staff expertise, and fleeting enthusiasm—are the seedbed for creative innovation. Why discourage these conditions? This is a bit like forbidding backyard vegetable gardens because they cannot produce cash crops to feed the whole nation.

In some cases, the demand for scalability might be linked to control, since large-scale innovations can be better mandated, measured, and marketed, allowing someone to take the credit or make profit. But leaders at the matrix level of the school system are usually more concerned about what works in the here and now. Not all entrepreneurial innovations are scalable; that doesn't mean they are not valuable. In short, the emphasis on scalability might reflect a determination to eliminate loose coupling, which we have found is conducive to innovation. There's nothing wrong with the *bricoleur* entrepreneur; most entrepreneurial effort is at this scale—and should be encouraged.

The other way to think about innovation is to identify the *conditions* for innovation and try to duplicate them everywhere. Let local educators unleash countless promising innovations, scalable or not, and let them flourish everywhere. Remember Picasso's dictum: "Good artists copy, great artists steal." There is no need to insist that every local innovation be entirely new and unique. There is real value in spreading the word about successful innovations, but rather than mandating undeviating implementation, why not encourage the people on the ground to own the idea and make their own adjustments? This approach is far more likely to result in optimal strategies for kids.

Scalability might be the word metric for educational innovations. Rather than replicability and scalability, perhaps we should emphasize diversity, multiplicity, adaptability, and applicability.

Long before I discovered my love for urban education, I was a college biology major and, later, a biology teacher. My favorite courses were the ones that took me outside to the ponds, swamps, mountains, and seacoast of New England. I was forever awed by the richness, diversity, and creativity of untouched nature. There were so many life forms to be found at every level, whether exploring the tidal lines on a deserted beach or looking through a dissecting microscope at the complex worlds growing on a strand of algae.

After finding my way to Dunbar High School, I read *The Race to Save the Lord God Bird* and was reminded again of the marvels of ecology.[14] The author lavished love on the swampy forests of Louisiana and reminded the reader of how man's shortsighted intrusions can violate the delicate balance with ruinous results, as in this case, with the extinction of a magnificent bird. This was the beginning of my interest in the *ecology* of education.

There's another forest that I pass in my travels; this one is a white pine forest in New Brunswick, which features miles and miles of similarly sized white pine trees planted in even rows, no doubt by some Canadian pulp company. I compared the endless sameness of the tree farm with the diversity and biological richness of the Louisiana swamps. This forest is a credit to the company's determination to replace trees, but it offers nowhere near the same productivity as the Louisiana forest. The undergrowth is lacking, the animal life is limited, and the total oxygen output is less. If the goal is simply to replace the trees that were chopped down with more pulpwood, then the New Brunswick forest is a success, but if the goal is productivity and healthfulness at every level, from the insect world to climate change, then the Louisiana forest is far and away superior.[15]

There is a severe price to be paid for leveling the rain forests of public education and replacing them with private enterprises and scalable products. Whenever I hear the story of the Great Lord God Bird and I picture the rich swamps of Louisiana, I am impressed again with the advantages of an ecological approach. Things grow of their own nature. You don't have to juice them with fertilizer, level all the habitats so they are identical, and force them with light. Plants, like kids, tend to grow naturally, exuberantly, wildly, richly. Leadership for the educational environment should begin with this premise: that kids want to learn and grow and adults/teachers want to teach, they want to get positive results, they want to see progress. They don't have to be driven. I fear we are destroying our educational environment in the same way we are recklessly attacking our natural environment.

The school that is an entrepreneurial organization is more like the Louisiana swamp forest than the New Brunswick replacement pine plots. The entrepreneurial organization is messy, somewhat unpredictable, and, yes, loosely coupled with a matrix-like organizational chart. The participants play different roles in this phenomenon. Teachers are often the intrapreneurs, creating adaptive innovations at the classroom level. The school principal may also be an intrapreneur, introducing new systems and approaches that better address the needs of students and teachers, but not all principals are entrepreneurial, as the case study of Compact Ventures will demonstrate. What is indispensable, however, for the entrepreneurial organization is a *cultural* leader who uses an ecologically sensitive approach to safeguard the process and products of innovation.

A good principal understands that an organization is like an individual, with its own history, identity, self-image, stability, and trajectory. The principal is an element in the organization in the same way that the head of the anatomical human body is an important but hardly independent element. Far too many leadership books—even those that have long since abandoned the "great man" theories of leadership—end up being about the individual and how he or she can be more transformational, more instructional, or more charismatic in leading the organization. *Cultural* leadership is a good name for leadership in the ecology of education.

## WHAT ABOUT THE PRINCIPAL?

One thing that was missing in the case study of Compact Ventures at Dunbar High School was the principal. And, in some ways, that was the point. The principal was not the innovation-generator. He was not the intrapreneur. But, he presided over an entrepreneurial organization. What can we learn from this case study?

Stanley Cohen (not his real name) was a health instructor, basketball coach, and assistant headmaster (a standard leadership résumé in those days) before he became the school principal in 1982. Cohen had smart strategic instincts, which were visible from the beginning. He won over the faculty with operational and cosmetic changes that addressed their concerns. For example, he tightened up school discipline, brought in the first school police, and insisted on better attendance. Even the students admired his leadership:

> He was very strict but he was very good. He was excellent. . . . I liked the way he handled the matters that came about. He handled them quick. He didn't waste any time. And he was very direct. If you were a troublemaker or causing problems, you were suspended right there. He didn't play games. Everybody knew it and I think that's why things ran so well. . . . But on the other hand, he would find time . . . like I was on the softball team and he came out and he watched us play our games. He didn't have to do that. So he was involved on both ends, like discipline but he was also there to encourage and to motivate and you know that was nice. You don't find that all the time.[16]

Cohen also found money and addressed badly needed building repairs, including new windows and new lockers for the students. As a result, students and staff supported him.

Cohen was fortunate because he began his term under a strong superintendent who had a plan for urban school reform, which included magnet programs under the Boston Compact. Cohen was able to use these ideas effectively at DHS. Wisely, he turned to the community partners for help. The PIC provided summer jobs, UMass Boston supported students through Upward Bound, and with help from New England Telephone, Cohen began a public relations blitz. UMass Boston and New England Telephone teamed up around the Compact Ventures initiative. The community partners enhanced Cohen's leadership, both privately and publicly. This deft coordination of resources that facilitated experimentation was part of Cohen's big-picture cultural leadership.

Cohen had a core of seasoned teacher leaders on his faculty. Louis and Miles called them "the class of '69," since most of them joined the staff in that year. The group included the chairs of the mathematics and science departments, a business teacher, a guidance counselor, and an assistant headmaster. They first developed their voice as school leaders in the 1970s, but their proactive leadership was essential for many of the innovations of the 1980s. The researchers noted, "This group seemed to share a personal affinity and a common view of how education should work. . . . They favored a humanistic approach that stressed individualization of learning experiences."[17] Rather than view the team's creativity as a threat, Cohen favored an ecological approach and encouraged their innovations.

The description of Louis and Miles will help us understand how this cultural leader preserved and promoted an entrepreneurial organization:

> [He] was far from being the charismatic "mover and shaker" figure that is often lauded in media accounts of school turnarounds. Rather, using an evolutionary strategy, he exhibited tenacity, flexibility, supportiveness, good problem-analysis and problem-solving skills, and a constant pressure on staff to take small steps, along with a tolerance for setbacks. His style is not that of the stereotyped masculine decisionmaker, but that of a nurturing- and demanding- parent.[18]

One can see the readiness for experimentation, risk-taking, and forgiveness evident in this analysis. The researchers summed up his careful approach: "The slower you go, the faster you get there."[19]

Cohen was not a larger-than-life superhero.[20] I interviewed teachers who served under his tenure. Teachers and students appreciated the positive climate that prevailed in the school under his reign but expressed no deep admiration for him personally. To some, he excelled in public relations both with the media and with central administration. Others admired him as a "smooth maneuverer," which reflected his deft political skills. One teacher showed some disdain at his attempts to institute curricular reform without any evident knowledge of the field. Another mid-level administrator dismissed his leadership, claiming that he came up with none of the innovations. The teachers and partners had done all the creative work.

To summarize, Dunbar was entrepreneurial in the 1980s because of the innovative efforts of the teachers and community partners, but we find that these were encouraged and facilitated by the skillful organizational leadership of the principal. Compact Ventures was just one among many victories for this school in the mid-1980s. Like the Louisiana swamp forest, the school was brimming with rich and diverse varieties of innovative growth. As the *School Profiles* revealed, Dunbar HS experienced an across-the-board renaissance at this time. The school's trophy cabinet was top-heavy with sports awards from that time period. The school yearbooks, which chronicled school culture year-by-year for over fifty years, were thick, cheerful, and colorful testimonies to the student joy and pride in that time period, in contrast to the depressing versions just a few years later. This was in addition to the academic accomplishments described earlier.

## CULTURAL REFORM STRATEGY

Cohen's cultural leadership contrasted with other school reform strategies. The analysis of the 1980 events at Dunbar High led to the discovery of a cultural reform strategy.[21] Historically, school reform initiatives have focused on curriculum or structures, since these are things that are measurable and somewhat controllable from the vantage point of central administration. When student achievement is lagging, it is easier to mandate a new curriculum or restructure the school than to address deeper, harder-to-manage issues such as culture. The curriculum and structure can be changed quickly, while school culture typically takes years to turn around.

As a result of curricular initiatives, the students at Dunbar had lost their art classes and physical education classes by the 1980s and were doubling up on English and reading. This is not dissimilar to the curricular aberrations found today under the national No Child Left Behind educational legislation (NCLB). In our terminology, curricular changes could include new math textbooks, a discovery-oriented science pedagogy, readers' or writers' workshop methodologies, integrated humanities classes, or even the incorporation of technology.

In Boston in the 1980s, there were also centrally mandated structural reforms, such as magnet school programs, which were a response to "white flight" and decreasing student enrollments. Other structural reforms in subsequent years have included block scheduling, an extended school day or year, K–8 or 6–12 school configurations, or small learning communities. There is a deceptive allure to structural reforms, which appear bold and decisive on the surface but often fall short of the desired results unless there is local buy-in. The limitations of restructuring were addressed in chapter 3.

While curricular and structural approaches to school reform hold promise, they are insufficient by themselves to change attitudes and practices on the ground. If the teachers and students do not own and implement the innovations at the ground level, they will have little impact. The research literature is rife with examples of such changes that lost impact on the ground. A cultural reform strategy takes the opposite approach and says, "Empower the teachers. Let them own the innovative processes." This strategy aims to shape school culture toward a more entrepreneurial organization.

This chapter offered a number of critical elements behind the successful decade of the 1980s at Dunbar High, where structural and curricular reforms were combined with a cultural reform strategy. There was outside pressure for measurable change, a consortium of community partners, a flexible vessel for school reform (in the Boston Compact), strong leadership from central administration, and an evolutionary planning strategy. The headmaster was not remembered for innovation; unlike the entrepreneurial leaders described in the early chapters of this book, he was not inventive. Instead, he oversaw an entrepreneurial organization. Under his leadership, and with support and encouragement from outside partners, DHS started to become an innovative learning organization.

Cohen was not remembered as a transformational leader, but the net effect was a transformation of the school culture. Teachers were excited by the empowerment. As evidence of the enthusiastic voluntarism, the teachers met every day to ensure the success of Compact Ventures. They had ownership of the thing they had invented, and they were excited to see positive outcomes. The students were motivated by the new attention and responded appropriately. The success came not because a structure or curriculum was superimposed on the staff and students; on the contrary, the staff and students created the new structure and the altered integrated curriculum. The shift in culture—to one of trust, empowerment, and collaboration—brought renewed energy and positive results.

Cultural reform theory means preserving the local in the face of an onslaught of federal, state, or district mandates. It means preserving safety—for teachers and students—with space for experimentation without fear of reprisal and room for innovation without worrying about scale. This is a decision, a vision for organizational learning, which is achieved on the ground. The research literature often mentions culture as an important factor, but top education leaders easily overlook it because they cannot conceive of a top-down way to dictate culture.

Cultural reform strategy is about getting the best out of teachers and students, empowering them for sustained work, and opening their minds to creative partnerships and innovation. Bryk and Schneider found that trust was the "key resource" for school improvement in their study of the Chicago public schools. They distinguished *contractual* trust, in which teachers and administrators could trust one another to fulfill the terms of the bargaining contract, from *relational* trust, whereby the talents and energy of teachers were released in innovative ways that went way beyond the terms of the contract.[22] This level of voluntarism is essential for school improvement and is only possible under a cultural reform strategy.

Relational trust is even more important with teenagers, especially in an inner city high school. The lack of engagement of teenagers in their own learning is well documented,[23] but this contrasts with the breathtaking energy they display when planning their school prom, or playing on a basketball team, or just meeting up with friends after school. In fact, young people have enormous energy and creative talents, which are too often neglected and wasted in school. Really good teachers know how to release these talents in the classroom. They use a combination of curricular and cultural reform strategies behind their classroom door. Compact Ventures employed a cultural reform strategy with at-risk ninth graders. This strategy included not only things that would maximize learning in the classroom but other things that would motivate students to come to school every day, to drop the chip on the shoulder, and to think as if they might become lifelong learners.

Cultural reform is not an overnight success strategy. Louis and Miles, who compared six high schools across the nation undergoing reform efforts, emphasized, "The slower you go, the faster you get there."[24] Compact Ventures was a success, but these students did not go on to Harvard. The work was slow and experimental. Students cannot be "jump-started" any more than a clock can be sped up with more voltage. Far too much of the national conversation is focused on how the public school can be turned around, jump-started, or even replaced as if this were nothing more than a local hardware store or laundromat in need of a new location or fresh marketing approach, instead of a community of young people.

There is a place for releasing students, and they often surprise us by their incredible ability to rise to the challenge, as was seen in the early college experiments in chapter 2, but students are not gasoline engines to be jump-started with a good shove. Schools that are serious about success need to lengthen their organizational attention span.[25]

The 1980s Compact Ventures case was not a complete success. The economic recession of 1988–1992 caused the PIC to re-evaluate their commitment to public education and also wiped out government support for Compact Ventures, so it disappeared. The initiative was not economically sustainable even though cultural reform is usually resilient through economic setbacks.

The gains at DHS were undermined by leadership transitions more than budgetary losses. Cohen left in 1988; his successor, who served as an assistant principal under Cohen, was unable to lead the cultural reform strategy. In a sense, Cohen failed to achieve "Level 5" leadership,[26] for he was unable to institute an enduring *leadership* culture in the principal's office. Nevertheless, not all was lost. Some members of the "class of '69" remained. Three teachers, who began experimenting with another magnet program in 1985, went on to create one of the most successful small learning communities in the city in the 1990s, despite the recession and the changes in leadership. Cohen's legacy and the cultural reforms lived on in one corner of the high school. The story is told in chapter 5.

## PHASE TWO AT DUNBAR

Twenty years later, I was the principal. Dunbar HS became small learning communities in the 1990s and then three small independent schools in 2003, one of which was mine. Whereas the 1980s were marked by an evolutionary planning strategy, which allowed for local expression, the twenty-first century felt more like a top-down implementation strategy where learning outcome goals and the processes to achieve these goals were determined outside the school at the district or state levels.[27] At that time, instructional leadership was the style-de-jour, and we were employed to make sure English teachers implemented readers' and writers' workshops, the science teachers had discovery-oriented classrooms, and the math teachers utilized collaborative learning techniques.

I came to the principalship, like Cohen, after serving as an assistant headmaster in the same building. Also, like Cohen, I came to leadership in a school that was on the upswing, although we were still ranked not far from the bottom of the pack among the city's high schools. Unlike Cohen, I had studied the history of the high school, looking back over fifty years as part of my doctoral dissertation. I paid particular attention to the school culture. I had also read the book by Louis and Miles, so I had some strong ideas about what worked and what didn't work historically with these teachers and this population.

One friend who ran several successful high schools and first got me thinking about entrepreneurial leadership told me that his secret to hiring personnel was to look for "half-glass-full" people. The analogy speaks for itself.[28] Entrepreneurial leaders refuse to see the world as a half-empty glass. We decided to take the same approach and see our school as half-full.

Our school was located in one of Boston's "murder zones," where police maps indicated a high rate of homicide. The local rates of poverty and teen pregnancy were among the highest in the city. Near the bottom of the city's thirty high schools, our school was one of the least selected in Boston's controlled choice program. No sensible parent would send their child through this neighborhood. There were lots of negatives.

When others were grousing about state-mandated achievement tests and regional competition from charter schools, we decided to focus on the things we could affect inside our school. I was an avid reader, so I knew that the whole world was testing their kids; this threat was not going away. I also knew that charter schools were driven, in part, by consumer choice, which would never diminish either. The half-glass-full approach freed us to concentrate on the things we could change.

Entrepreneurial leaders tend to be out-of-the-box thinkers. This is more than just an analogy. To be entrepreneurial, one has to get out of the box. The physical building can be a box, a depressing one at times when the facility is eighty years old. More importantly, the bureaucratic hierarchy of public education, in any district, is an insidious box, which can dominate one's attention and threaten originality.

The entrepreneurial leader has to find ways to get outside the box. There are many ways to do this. Meeting with colleagues across the district—anyone outside one's own school—is a step in the right direction. Fortunately, a large district includes a lot of alternative voices. We met with other high school leaders; we also met with elementary and middle school leaders so we could think about alignment and recruitment issues.

In addition, we began meeting with community partners in higher education, business, health, social services, youth services, and philanthropy. We built partnerships with UMass Boston and Bunker Hill Community College. We partnered with TJX Companies, Sovereign Bank, Verizon, and the City Lights Electrical Company and offered business internships to our students. We networked with the Trefler Foundation, Nellie Mae, and the Woodrow Wilson Foundation. Other partners included Teen Empowerment and the neighborhood health centers. At every stop, we were unabashed (Kirznerian) opportunists. Outside partners are a wonderful way to gain new perspective, which will be considered again in chapter 6.

Reading about education in other districts, systems, and countries is a great help. One can accept that charter schools are a threat, for example, or one can learn from them. We chose to learn and imitate (or as Picasso would say, "steal") some of their ideas, such as the extended school day, the widespread incorporation of technology, and student advisories. Some of the best school leaders I have known often have a leadership book under their arm, many of which were written for the business environment, not schooling.

## PROFESSIONAL DEVELOPMENT

This book cites literature by Rosabeth Moss Kanter, Jim Collins, Peter Senge, Ron Heifetz, Marty Linsky, and others, many of whom have ties to Harvard Business School. I read the HBR blog network regularly. Every time I cite Steven Denning or Scott Anthony or anyone who might be found on the HBR network, I cringe, knowing that someone will accuse me of neoliberalism, selling out to the corporate agenda, or taking a business approach to education.

Stereotypical labels can cripple creative thinking. Business people study leadership because they know that a lot is at stake in their enterprises. We have even more at stake, for while they value profits, we value children. This means all the more reason to read everything on leadership available. In some cases, the business leaders are way ahead of us in their discussion of ethics and organizational culture as well. Social entrepreneurship is a hot topic in business circles.

As public school leaders, we should consider carefully what commands our attention. If our nose is to the grindstone all the time, then we will become grindstone experts and nothing else. Everything we touch will become a grindstone, including our school.

Business experts have lots of advice for how school principals can build entrepreneurial cultures that unleash creativity and innovation. Obviously, inviting experimentation, tolerating failure, forgiving mistakes, and all the "enabling behaviors" described in chapter 3 are important. Experts also point out that the use of time can be an important factor. For example, Red Gate is a software company, which recognizes that a change of pace is good for creative thinking. Their annual schedule is built to promote entrepreneurism. They sponsor an annual "down tools" week, which invites company workers to set aside routine work to spend time on intriguing problems, risky ideas, or just something new that has been waiting for attention. This is an open invitation to explore. On the other hand, they also schedule a "sweat the small stuff" day each quarter, which allows employees to catch up on bureaucratic requirements or nagging duties. In this way, everyone is able to relax and return to more imaginative work. [29]

There is some evidence that school principals would like to learn how to lead an entrepreneurial institution. In one study, 250 head teachers in Scotland were surveyed; nearly 75 percent indicated that they would like professional development on "how to lead an enterprising and innovative school." [30] However, in the United States only a few graduate programs make a deliberate effort to train entrepreneurial leaders in education. For example, the Rice University Education Entrepreneurship Program (REEP) combines business school courses with a traditional educational administration curriculum to equip entrepreneurially minded school leaders. [31] Other venues, such as the Ritchie Program for School Leaders in the Morgridge College of Education at the University of Denver, offer a specific course titled "Entrepreneurial Leadership." [32] The opportunities are limited, so some non-profits, such as Louisiana's Advance Innovative Education, offer to work with school principals to turn them into social entrepreneurs. [33]

## CONCLUSION

Therefore, despite the emphasis from the superintendent's office and Washington, DC, we adopted a cultural reform strategy at Dunbar High School, promoting student empowerment, encouraging teacher leadership, and pulling in strategic community partners. We didn't wait for partners to show up and provide leadership; we lined up partners, aggressively. We led.

Our goal was to become a learning organization with an eye out for innovations that worked for everyone. Whereas the cultural reform strategy had been effective locally in Compact Ventures and other isolated pockets of excellence in the school in the 1980s, we attempted to take this school-wide in the 2000s. I had taught courses at UMass Boston on action research, so experimentation, risk-taking, and measurement were in my blood. One year, we even had all our teachers collaborate on action research projects.

As a small school, our theme was business, but our real theme was learning. I told my students and staff all the time, "We are in the business of learning. If we are not lifelong learners, then who will be?" I found I had little tolerance for educators who stopped learning. Of course, this kind of leadership requires a certain amount of transparency, as Elmore says,

> If learning, individual and collective, is the central responsibility of leaders, then they must be able to model the learning they expect of others. Leaders should be doing, and should be seen to be doing, that which they expect or require others to do. Likewise, leaders should expect to have their own practice subjected to the same scrutiny as they exercise toward others. [34]

Using the cultural reform strategy, we worked with students, staff, and partners to develop shared ownership of a learning organization that was constantly experimenting, innovating, and adapting. In the face of absenteeism, violence, and a high dropout rate, we brought in mental health counselors and doubled up on the social workers on our staff. We reinstituted the arts and resuscitated the physical education program. We found a way to get breakfast into the hands of every student, even when they were chronically late to school. We toured eighth graders through the school to dispel their fears, and we paid them to attend summer school with us so they would be fully acclimated on the first day in September. We lengthened the school day for our ninth graders and developed incentives for academic success. We sent our juniors out on student internships in the business community. Every senior learned how to fill out applications for college and financial aid; as a result, every graduate had at least one acceptance letter is his/her portfolio. This was just a handful of the many innovations.

I was an unremarkable leader. I won no awards. I was not a Ralph Spezio by any means, but I do think we had an entrepreneurial school. David Bornstein, in his cutting-edge book on social entrepreneurship, described the willingness of these leaders to self-correct. Rather than being stuck on a plan (or mesmerized by their own ego), they were attached to a goal and willing to change course when necessary. [35] When I was principal, I spent six months courting the teachers with a new block schedule that I thought would make it easier for our students to participate in after-school activities such as dual enrollment. The teachers overwhelmingly rejected the proposal. There were many reasons, historically, contextually, and maybe personally, why they did not always trust my leadership. We found other ways to send our students off to college courses.

Within two years of working together, we were a finalist for Boston's EdVestors award for school improvement and took home a $25,000 prize. The following year, we were *number one in the state* for improvement on the state-mandated student achievement tests. The state commissioner of education, superintendent of schools, and the mayor all visited us that day. The next year, we won a lucrative four-year grant for expanded after-school programs. Despite the fact that our school still lingered in the bottom 50 percent on district metrics, we were moving in the right direction.

There were other failures. Like Cohen, twenty years earlier, I was unable to craft a leadership succession plan, but I left behind a cadre of teacher leaders who continued to pull the school in the right direction. These teachers were familiar with the power of experimentation and innovation.

I believe entrepreneurial leadership is moral leadership. Fundamentally, the entrepreneurial leader is willing to say, "This is not working," and push for better solutions. This leader is not satisfied with the achievement gap, bullying, school shootings, disparities, inequities, the dropout rate, high teacher turnover, or a hundred other obvious problems. This leader is not satisfied with tiny, incremental improvements or to just be better than the next school. There is a fundamental dissatisfaction, a restlessness that demands new ways of thinking without blaming, scapegoating, or taking shortcuts.

Entrepreneurial leadership breathes hope. This is inspirational leadership—not because of a charismatic leader stirring the emotions but because entrepreneurial organizations provoke people to dream again, to imagine, to create, and to act. There is no sense in challenging the status quo, no reason for all the experimenting, the risk-taking, and the three-steps-forward-and-two-steps-back pathway unless we hope—believe—that there are innovations out there that will help our teachers and our students succeed today.

Critics will carp that the ideas presented in these chapters are simplistic and shortsighted; they will consider my understanding shallow. No doubt, they are right in part. The point is that we are presenting ideas, which are the lifeblood of the entrepreneur. Possibility thinking. Daring to imagine the new. Entrepreneurial leaders are not hung up on "ifs, ands, or buts"; they are more intrigued with where the next idea could lead. They see the glass as half-full instead of half-empty.

People need hope to live, and those who work and learn in the most trying situations need plenty of hope. Most of all, the entrepreneurial leader embodies a vision of a better world. In the 1960s President John F. Kennedy inspired the nation with his call for sacrifice: "Ask not what your country can do for you, but what you can do for your country." He pointed to the moon and gave us an unbelievable target. His leadership added meaning and dimension to our mundane lives. Today, fifty years later, we wrestle with a multi-trillion-dollar national deficit, climate change, and a growing suspicion that our nation is trailing the world in education, children's health, prison reform, women's rights, and many other social and economic indicators. Our airwaves are filled with dire extremism. The need for hope is stronger than ever.

Common sense leadership books tell us to set achievable goals. Strategic leaders go after the "low-hanging fruit" and, where possible, offer technical solutions to build staff confidence. Then, they set more challenging, but achievable goals to spur on the team. But Vijay Govindarajan urges leaders to set unrealistic goals. "Realistic goals promote incremental moves; only unrealistic goals provoke breakthrough thinking."[36] This is entrepreneurial leadership.

Our teachers and students come to school day after day, dutifully working toward a better world. Teachers make daily sacrifices, hoping against hope that their lives make a difference. Students slog through, hoping that at the end of all this studying, these tests and countless assignments, they too will enjoy the life of their dreams. While they may never express the desire in so many words, they long for inspiration, someone to remind them of why they come. They long for hope.

People ache for moral leadership. Not the kind of blaming, narrowing, constricting moral leadership that boxes people in, but moral leadership that leads us back to the values we all embrace at a deeper level—leadership that awakens the best in each of us. As leaders, we can't afford to let ourselves get buried under problems and not offer hope, leadership, vision, a way out, and a way forward to our friends.

## NOTES

1. Much of the historical information regarding Dunbar High School comes from Leonard, J. (2002). History of a high school community, 1950–2000 (Massachusetts). *DAI, 63*(02A), 318.

2. Gonsalves, L., & Leonard, J. (2007). *New hope for urban high schools: Cultural reform, moral leadership and community partnership.* Westport, CT: Praeger; Leonard, J. (2002). History of a high school community, 1950–2000 (Massachusetts). *DAI, 63*(02A), 318; Louis, K. S., & Miles, M. B. (1990). *Improving the urban high school: What works and why.* New York: Teachers College Press.

3. Leonard, J. (2002). History of a high school community, 1950–2000 (Massachusetts). *DAI, 63*(02A), 318; Leonard, J. (2009). Using Bronfenbrenner's ecological theory to understand community partnerships: An historical case study of one urban high school. *Urban Education.*

4. National Commission on Excellence in Education. (1983). *A nation at risk: The imperative for educational reform* (p. 65). Washington, DC: US Department of Education.

5. Clarence Stone set the standard for research on citywide partnerships: Stone, C. N. (2001). Civic capacity and urban education. *Urban Affairs Review, 36*(5), 595–619; Stone, C. N. (Ed.). (1998). *Changing urban education.* Lawrence: University Press of Kansas.

6. Louis, K. S., & Miles, M. B. (1990).

7. Louis, K. S., & Miles, M. B. (1990), 65.

8. Sege, I. (1985, June 29). Year over, freshmen in [Dilmotte] a step ahead. *The Boston Globe*, p. 1.

9. Louis, K. S., & Miles, M. B. (1990), 73–74.

10. Anthony, S. (2012, May 22). The Mount Rushmore of innovation, para. 6. Retrieved from http://blogs.hbr.org/anthony/2012/05/the_mount_rushmore_of_innovati.html.

11. BPS. (1984). *School profiles.* Boston: Boston Public Schools, 133–134.

12. Tucker, M. (2011, December 6). Why innovation can't fix America's classrooms. *The Atlantic.*

13. Hess, F. M. (2007). *Reimagining American schooling: The case for educational entrepreneurship* (Vol. 4). Washington, DC: American Enterprise Institute for Public Policy Research; Hess, F. M. (2011, December 5). Why education innovation tends to crash and burn. Retrieved from http://blogs.edweek.org/edweek/rick_hess_straight_up/2011/12/why_education_innovation_tends_to_crash_and_burn.html.

14. Hoose, P. M. (2004). *The race to save the Lord God Bird* (1st ed.). New York: Farrar, Straus and Giroux.

15. My apologies to New Brunswick, which certainly has many other wild and wonderful natural forests in this large province.

16. Leonard, J. (2002), quoting Edwards, M. (2000). Interview.

17. Louis, K. S., & Miles, M. B. (1990), 60.

18. Louis, K. S., & Miles, M. B. (1990), 77.

19. Louis, K. S., & Miles, M. B. (1990), 77.

20. Other leadership scholars have also tried to describe this kind of low-key leadership. Michael Fullan called it spiritual leadership and summarized some findings in this short article in *The School Administrator* (Fullan, 2002, para. 16–19):

> Little of the above will happen if we idealize spiritual leadership. For one thing, charismatic, visionary leadership is the wrong conception for getting the job done. Second, only a few exceptional people meet this idealized standard. Again recent studies bear out a more accessible, humble image of leaders at many levels.
>
> Collins, in his book, found that charismatic leaders were negatively associated with sustainable performance. The 11 leaders who built enduring greatness were not high-profile flashy performers but rather "individuals who blend extreme personal humility with intense professional will."
>
> Joseph Badaracco, in his 2002 book *Leading Quietly*, makes a similar case. Leaders who do the right thing lead quietly. They are at all levels of the organization and do not necessarily stand out. They are not spiritual in terms of God-like

purity, but are all too human as they recognize "mixed motives" in themselves. They don't try to "save the world," or "buy time" (especially when problems are complex), nor do they "bend the rules" and "craft compromises," according to Badaracco, a professor at the Harvard Business School. These leaders exemplify what he calls "three quiet virtues"—restraint, modesty and tenacity.

Richard Farson and Ralph Keyes provide a similar portrayal in *Whoever Makes the Most Mistakes Wins*. Such leaders are not preoccupied by looking good, but rather by learning from efforts to solve complex problems. Ronald Heifetz and Marty Linsky, co-authors of *Leadership on the Line*, also give a more realistic image of "staying alive through the dangers of leading." Their last chapter is titled "Sacred Heart" in which three virtues are discussed—innocence, curiosity and compassion. These virtues tap into our deeper sense of purpose, but not in a high-falutin way. Once again spirituality plays itself out in humble, messy circumstances.

21. Gonsalves, L., & Leonard, J. (2007).

22. Bryk, A. S., & Schneider, B. L. (2002). *Trust in schools: A core resource for improvement*. New York City: Russell Sage Foundation.

23. Steinberg, L., Brown, B. B., & Dornbusch, S. M. (1996). *Beyond the classroom: Why school reform has failed and what parents need to do*. New York: Simon and Schuster.

24. Louis, K. S., & Miles, M. B. (1990), 77.

25. Hamel, G., & Prahalad, C. K. (1989). Strategic intent. *Harvard Business Review, 67*(3), 63–78.

26. Collins, J. (2001). *Good to great: Why some companies make the leap . . . and others don't*. New York: Harper Business.

27. Louis, K. S., & Miles, M. B. (1990).

28. Murray, L. (2012). Personal communication.

29. Birkinshaw, J. (2012, November 7). Taming your company's elusive beast. Retrieved from http://blogs.hbr.org/cs/2012/11/three_rules_for_making_innovat.html.

30. Woods, P. A. (2012). *The purpose of educational leadership: Reconfiguring entrepreneurialism in public education*, p. 6. Paper presented at the Annual Convention of the University Council for Educational Administration, Denver, CO.

31. Rice/REEP. (2013). Retrieved February 25, 2013, from http://business.rice.edu/reep.aspx.

32. Ritchie Program for School Leaders. Retrieved February 25, 2013, from http://www.du.edu/education/programs/leadership/ritchie/.

33. Hebert, K., Bendickson, J., Liguori, E. W., Weaver, K. M., & Teddlie, C. (2012). Re-designing lessons, re-envisioning principals: Developing entrepreneurial school leadership. In K. Sanzo, S. Myran, & A. H. Normore (Eds.), *Successful School Leadership Preparation and Development* (Vol. 17, pp. 153–163). Bingley, West Yorkshire, England: Emerald Group Publishing Limited.

34. Elmore, R. F. (2000). *Building a new structure for school leadership* (p. 42). Washington, DC: The Albert Shanker Institute, 21.

35. Bornstein, D. (2004). *How to change the world: Social entrepreneurs and the power of new ideas*. New York: Oxford University Press.

36.  Govindarajan, V. (2012, October 22). The Timeless Strategic Value of Unrealistic Goals, para. 4. Retrieved from http://blogs.hbr.org/govindarajan/2012/10/the-timeless-strategic-value-of-unrealistic-goals.html.

# 5

# THE ENTREPRENEURIAL
# TEACHER LEADER

Teacher leadership has been a topic of interest for over twenty-five years, so there is a lot of commendable writing on the traits, roles, benefits, development, growth, and history of teacher leadership. However, the literature on the contribution of teacher leadership to school entrepreneurism is scarce.

This chapter postulates that there is a reciprocal relationship between teacher leadership and entrepreneurial schools. When the school operates like an entrepreneurial organization (as described in chapter 3), then teacher leadership is released and everyone, including students, benefits. This happens for several reasons. First, teachers are better positioned to accept and incorporate *inherited* innovations. This includes new initiatives, which may have been selected by the school, district, or even state, such as common core curriculum standards or a new literacy program or the introduction of computer tablets. An entrepreneurial organization is more agile; teachers are provided with favorable conditions that facilitate adaptation, adoption, and implementation.

Teachers are also better positioned for *invented* innovations in an entrepreneurial organization. In other words, the characteristics of the entrepreneurial environment release teacher leaders to create custom-tailored innovations that address local problems in their own classroom, department, school, or neighborhood. In both respects, the entrepreneurial organization helps everyone adjust to change more easily.

Teacher leadership and organizational entrepreneurism are reciprocally related, so the development of one can enhance the other. School principals who want to run a more entrepreneurial school should focus on the development of teacher leadership. As this chapter shows, this is easier said than done.


## WHAT IS TEACHER LEADERSHIP?

Teacher leaders come in all shapes and sizes, from exemplary classroom instructors to mentors and coaches, department chairs, union representatives, and committee heads. While no list is absolutely definitive, most teacher leaders share some of the following characteristics. [1]

They tend to be very good teachers. Federal and state attention to teaching outcomes, as measured by student achievement and classroom climate, makes this an increasingly important indicator. Even teachers admit that they have less respect for a colleague who is in a leadership position but lacks skill in the classroom. [2]

Teacher leaders are often curious individuals for whom lifelong learning is more than a nice phrase in the school mission statement. They read all the time, they listen, and they learn from others; they are well-informed about their own practice as well as emerging trends in their field. These teachers reflect on their learning and on their practice. Many understand and regularly use action research strategies.

Teachers cannot be leaders unless they influence others, so teacher leaders also tend to be collegial. They build relationships with other teachers, parents, and community partners. Their influence extends beyond the classroom. In fact, many teachers begin to emerge as leaders when they gain a sense of mastery in their own classroom and begin to assume responsibility for the larger school.

Their leadership is not dominating or intimidating; instead, they empower others. Rather than being secretive and competitive, they are more likely to share best practices and willingly provide mentoring or coaching assistance, both formally and informally.

Their leadership is based upon trust, since unlike administrative leadership, these teachers have more assumed than assigned authority. In most systems, they cannot evaluate their peers; usually, they have no rewards and no coercive power. They have person power (referent and expert) rather than positional power. [3] For this reason, "developing trusting and collaborative relationships is the primary means by which teacher leaders influence their colleagues." [4]

Many teacher leaders exhibit distinctly entrepreneurial traits. Like Lynn Gatto, they target learning problems and are quick to create a better curriculum. Similar to social entrepreneurs, many bring advocacy skills to the job, working on the behalf of children or parents or other teachers. Researchers also point to specific entrepreneurial traits, such as a "willingness to take responsible risks"[5] or "the ability to use a variety of influence techniques to 'sell' their point of view."[6]

## AN EXAMPLE OF A TEACHER LEADER

Diana Christian was a former hospital lab technician who made a career change to become a science teacher in a tough urban high school. As a mother of teenagers, she was never intimidated by the edgy urban students, and the students loved her. She taught biology, chemistry, and introduced the first Advanced Placement course in her school.

Diana was the oldest member, by age, of the science department, and she took it upon herself to mentor the young beginning science teachers in the classrooms around her own. She observed their classes, helped them find lab equipment, and stayed with them after school. All this was part of building an exemplary science program. As she said, "Their students are going to come to my classroom in a few years; I want to make sure they're ready."

Over time, the entrepreneurial talents of this teacher emerged. The 1925 classroom she inherited was a barren space that had long since surrendered to student antipathy. Recruiting teams of students around her innovative ideas, Diana slowly changed the culture of the classroom and filled it with terrariums, fish bowls, microscopes, and countless samples of student experiments.

This science teacher regularly called parents to talk about her students, for both positive and constructive reasons. Mother-to-mother talks came easily to her. She was also comfortable talking to the state Biotechnology Council, which recognized her entrepreneurial innovativeness and donated nearly $10,000 in equipment to her classroom. As a result, her crowded classroom sported an incubator, UV-sterilizer, spectroscope, DNA electrophoresis dishes, and Winogradsky columns. In fact, the resources in her classroom surpassed the best exam schools in the city. They were regularly used by her students.

Her accomplishments were acknowledged across the district. The local university often invited Diana to lead summer classes for other city science teachers. This ability to reach across boundaries—between classrooms, between the faculty and administration, or between the school and the outside community—was an important quality. Diana was able to think outside the box. Several scholars have noted the boundary-spanning abilities of teacher leaders such as Diana.[7]

How teacher leaders achieve their position is not entirely understood, a topic that is taken up later in this chapter. However, it is important to note that the whole point of teacher leadership is *leadership*, not followership, sycophancy, imitation, or compliance. Teacher leadership is negotiated with colleagues and administrators.

In summary, there are many definitions of teacher leadership, depending on whom you ask and when you are asking, since the phenomenon has changed over the years. This is one of the best definitions since it emphasizes the behaviors and outcomes of teacher leaders, instead of just the character traits:

> Teacher leadership is the process by which teachers, individually or collectively, influence their colleagues, principals, and other members of the school communities to improve teaching and learning practices with the aim of increased student learning and achievement. Such team leadership work involves three intentional development foci: individual development, collaboration or team development, and organizational development. [8]

Teacher leaders are often spotlighted as individuals (such as Lynn Gatto and Diana Christian), but their real strengths lie in their leadership that shifts the organizational culture.

## A CASE STUDY: DUNBAR AGAIN

The Dunbar case study is illustrative. [9] When Stanley Cohen left Dunbar High School in 1988, simultaneously with the nation's slide into economic recession, the school slumped into a six-year dark period of slashed services and student violence. The media reported on the school shootings and student deaths, but there was a counter-narrative occurring in one corner of the school.

In the early 1980s many city high schools were developing magnet themes to counteract "white flight," and Dunbar was no exception. Frank Micciula submitted a proposal for a human services academy, which eventually emerged as the LEAP Academy, an acronym standing for a loose assembly of introductory courses in law, education, allied health and public service. Later in the decade, Boston's Private Industry Council approached one of Dunbar's English teachers, Paul Costello, with a proposal for a student program linked to a national consortium of public service academies. Costello drafted Micciula and another social studies teacher, John Rosotti.

The Private Industry Council introduced the teachers to the American Society of Public Administrators, which was spearheading similar academies across the country. With support from the PIC and other community partners, such as New England Telephone, the University of Massachusetts Boston, and even Harvard University, the three teachers got grounded in the new concept. They travelled to Chicago and New York to learn more and then met together over weekends to formulate their plans. Along the way, they secured the permission of the headmaster and, finally, the superintendent.

The new small learning community, called the Academy of Public Service, recruited its first cohort of tenth graders in 1991 and offered them a series of courses that focused on academic success and public administration. Getting into the academy was a big deal; students filled out applications, brought in letters of reference, and dressed up for the interview. Out of one hundred applications, only thirty-three students might be selected for a cohort. In many ways, this was their first taste of the competitive pathway toward college.

The Academy of Public Service (APS), which was introduced by a community partner and built by three teacher leaders, became the most significant program at Dunbar High School for the next ten years. This is especially significant when one considers the overall decline of the school. By the mid-1990s, Dunbar had the highest dropout rate of any comprehensive high school in the state. In 1996 the regional accrediting agency put the school on probation. The school was one of the least selected high schools in the city and was filled throughout the year with a stream of assigned students who came from broken homes (where no one was selecting a high school), from the city's youth detention center, or from the Caribbean islands. Remarkably, within this same time period, 95 percent of the APS graduates were going on to two- and four-year colleges.

Chapter 3 described how innovation can sometimes occur despite the organizational culture because there are holes or neglected areas in the organization. In many respects, this was the case with the birth of APS. Dunbar was dysfunctional and struggling with staffing issues. APS was an educational innovation created by a team of teachers in collaboration with community partners, which operated under the radar of the school administration.

In subsequent years, as the concept of the small learning community spread, Dunbar's organizational culture became more supportive. A new superintendent and headmaster began to pay attention to this pocket of success. Federal and state grant funds appeared for school restructuring and small learning communities.

A big break for APS came when Pam Trefler joined the advisory board. At one time, Pam was an aspiring teacher who attended classes at the University of Massachusetts Boston and served her teaching practicum under Costello's tutelage. But Trefler married a highly successful software developer and went on to oversee an endowed educational foundation. Her first gift to APS was $50,000 for scholarships and other basic needs.

With additional funds, APS came up with other innovations, including a "Strategies for Success" class to help students make the leap to college expectations and a dedicated computer writing lab (at a time when computer labs were still rare). Every student was linked with an adult mentor from the business community, who provided everything from career counseling to help with a dress for the upcoming prom.

The founding teachers met daily to integrate their courses, plan field trips and guest speakers, and monitor the progress of every student. They initiated quarterly award ceremonies, which were formal events in the school cafeteria to celebrate academic accomplishments with photographs and refreshments. The business mentors often attended. The PIC provided a full-time career specialist who met with the teachers and arranged internships and summer jobs for students, yet another strategy to build confidence and maturity. School administrators did not attend these meetings.

The Academy of Public Service became the standard for academic excellence at Dunbar High School, and students began competing to get into the program in the ninth grade. The teacher-driven small learning community approach was so successful that others were created in the late 1990s, so that by 2000 all students were enrolled in one community or another. Every community at Dunbar was designed, crafted, and run by a teacher leader. Visitors came from the other end of the country to learn how this urban high school had successfully restructured.

In 2003 the small school movement was sweeping across America with support from the Gates Foundation. [10] Dunbar High School, after 150 years of service, was broken up into three small, independent schools, one of which was the Academy of Public Service. The teachers' invention now became a full-fledged school. By this time, all three founders had retired.

Teacher leaders are often foremost in the development of an entrepreneurial organization. The initial innovation, crafted by three teacher leaders in the late 1980s, was replicated throughout the school. By the late 1990s, there was a significant and elaborate organizational network that was highly entrepreneurial. In this environment, at least five other teacher-designed and teacher-led small learning communities were created.

Furthermore, this story provides new understanding of the entrepreneurial network. The collaboration of the APS teachers with the school administrative staff, the superintendent's office, and the Trefler Foundation, in conjunction with targeted federal and state grants, suggests that the concept of a supportive organizational culture should be expanded beyond the confines of the school walls. The next chapter on school partnerships will develop this idea more fully.

Not all teacher leaders are entrepreneurs, for there are many styles of leadership and teacher leadership can take many forms. However, teacher leader entrepreneurism and an entrepreneurial organizational culture go hand-in-hand. Chapter 3 established that most productive entrepreneurial thinking comes from the middle of the organization, not the top. Local school teachers and principals are more likely than central office workers to be the source of creative approaches to education.

## A DIFFERENT KIND OF TEACHER LEADERSHIP

Years ago, a teacher named Jaime Escalante successfully coached hundreds of inner city Mexican kids through the Advanced Placement exam in calculus. He defied expectations and sent many students, whom others had dismissed, off to college. Hollywood created a movie called *Stand and Deliver*, and Escalante became a Superman figure and a kind of standard for the profession.[11] Escalante was a teacher leader, and he was certainly entrepreneurial, so he ought to be at the center of this chapter. There are, however, some cautionary notes in his story.

First, he worked tirelessly for so many hours—through weekends, over vacations—that he ruined his health. Frame-breaking leadership can require supreme sacrifices at times, and while Escalante's sacrifices are heroic, the salvation of public education should not demand this level of sacrifice. Too often, educational innovations are built on a level of sacrifice that is not sustainable. For example, too many new school startups depend on young, idealistic teachers to work long hours at poverty-level wages.

Escalante's innovation was disruptive to his students, the school, and to public education in general. This is not a criticism, but rather just something to keep in mind. Chapter 2 introduced a spectrum of entrepreneurial activity. At one end was the creative destruction of Joseph Schumpeter, and then along the spectrum were other opportunistic entrepreneurs who capitalized on the original creation. Clearly, Escalante was working toward the Schumpeter end of the spectrum. For this reason, he worked alone. Unlike the examples offered earlier, he was not a team player; in fact, some of his colleagues resented him. The overwhelming demands he placed on his students interfered with all kinds of other programs in the school, as well as students' schedules for home, jobs, and sports.

Eventually, lots of teachers imitated Escalante with a dream of getting a group of underachieving students through AP Calculus (or some other AP course). They were the Kirznerian imitators and opportunists. Escalante's innovation was truly scalable because it required little money, but just determination and hard work. No doubt, thousands of students have enjoyed a classroom with high expectations because of his example.

Too often, however, admiring teachers have mimicked the accomplishment, rather than the entrepreneurial imagination that prompted Escalante to ponder the "what-if" questions, to problem-solve and think outside the box. Escalante became a standard for high expectations and dedication, but not entrepreneurism. The erection of a standard can encourage imitation, but it can actually discourage innovation. Carl Rogers once wrote, "The very essence of the creative is its novelty, and hence we have no standard by which to judge it."[12]

In general, teacher leaders are not superheroes. Chapter 2 abandoned the magical model of heroic school leadership and found that entrepreneurial leaders were not necessarily powerful, charismatic, larger-than-life characters. The same can be said about teacher leaders. The point of this chapter is not to find the Clark Kent among all teachers and release the Escalante Superman. Contrary to the controversial documentary film *Waiting for Superman*, this book does not advocate waiting for a superhero to save public education.[13] The full spectrum of entrepreneurism is needed, which would include the occasional Schumpeterian Escalante disrupter and the many opportunistic imitators.

## A HISTORICAL LOOK

The concept of teacher leadership has evolved over the past thirty years, and this was true at Dunbar High School also.[14] In the 1980s teacher leaders tended to have formal positions within the school, such as department chair or lead teacher. Often, this was one step on the career ladder toward school or central administration. Teacher leadership was defined and called out by administrators who were higher up in the bureaucracy. For this reason, Frank Micciula, Paul Costello, and John Rosotti were not called teacher leaders in their early days.

An expanded view of teacher leadership came into play because of various whole-school reform movements, such as school-based management and professionalization.[15] Systemic reform was supported with large federal grant programs including Magnet Schools, Small Learning Communities, and Comprehensive School Reform Demonstration. All of these grants were important at Dunbar High School.

The 1990s brought a new focus on standards, accountability, student achievement, and instructional leadership. At this time, every principal was expected to be an instructional leader, and as a result, the best teachers were often drafted for key positions. Teachers led accreditation committees or, as at Dunbar, invented freshmen academies, small learning communities, or alternative academic programs. Sometimes, teachers led professional development with their colleagues or developed curriculum.

By 2000, however, educators began to understand the need for deeper change—cultural change—if there was to be real school improvement. The structural changes of the 1990s were a step in the right direction, but, as chapter 4 established, unless there was real teacher ownership of the reform initiatives, there was unlikely to be deep and permanent change in the school. A cultural reform strategy was necessary.

Across the country, educators began to challenge the isolating culture of the school, where teachers worked independently behind closed doors, with a more collaborative culture that promised shared participation and mutual learning. Professional learning communities (PLCs) emerged as one means to improve teaching and learning. In PLCs, teachers met, often without an administrator, to share challenges and best practices. They observed one another's instruction and provided a layer of peer coaching which was less threatening than the traditional performance evaluation.[16] The APS teachers met regularly as an informal, self-organized PLC.

Teacher leadership in the 1980s and 1990s was largely concerned with the overall administration and organization of the school, but the focus after 2000 returned to the classroom, since this is where "the rubber meets the road." Unless teaching and learning changed, all other efforts to boost budgets, launch initiatives, restructure the schools, change the curriculum, or try out new leadership approaches would be largely ineffective.

Today, PLCs offer an opportunity to shift the focus back onto what happens in the classroom. Teachers who remain in the profession often build their lesson plans and get on top of classroom management within a few years, but they might never develop the sophisticated skills of formative assessment and differentiated instruction without mentoring. PLCs present a means to step up the quality of teaching.

When a school is committed to a cultural reform strategy (see chapter 4), which includes targeted empowerment, the expansion of teacher leadership is an obvious and anticipated outcome. English Alma Harris concluded,

> It has been argued that creating supportive structures, including a collaborative environment, is the "single most important factor" for successful school improvement and "the first order of business" for those seeking to enhance the effectiveness of teaching and learning (Eastwood & Louis, 1992, p. 215). The findings from teacher leadership literature highlight how collegial relationships promote inquiry-orientated practice and generate an environment of continuous improvement. This effectively relinquishes the notion of structure as a means of control, viewing it rather as "a vehicle for empowering others" (Lambert, 1998).[17]

This paragraph argues that entrepreneurial activities, such as inquiry, problem-solving, and innovation, are the outcome when teacher leaders are empowered, resulting in whole school improvement. The author argues for an organizational culture that unleashes teacher talent, which is the opposite of great accountability and control.

## ECONOMIC AND SOCIAL DEFINITIONS

This twenty-first-century renewed focus on teaching marks a shift in the definition of teacher leadership and, in some cases, a shift from a *social* to a more *economic* understanding of entrepreneurial teacher leadership. The *economic* approach looks at schooling as an investment in the nation's work force. As much as possible, the work of teaching and learning is reduced to a set of metrics, which can be rewarded accordingly. Teachers are tested when they enter the profession, they are scrutinized in the performance of their job, student outcomes are measured with standardized achievement tests, and, in some cases, teachers are rewarded financially for the results. Some adherents of this neoliberal approach even believe that the surest route to international competitiveness is to circumvent traditional public institutions, investing instead in charter schools and alternative teacher and school leader preparation programs.

Entrepreneurship is often associated with the neoliberal agenda and, therefore, held up for suspicion. However, *social* entrepreneurship is committed to the public good instead of private profits. Included here is the belief that the public—which would include parents, students, and teachers—rather than corporations should define what constitutes the public good. An economic interpretation tends toward international comparisons and national standards and controls, while a social interpretation suggests a more local, democratic approach to public schooling.

In recent years, the renewed attention to the technical core of schooling has meant a tightening accountability regimen, which is antithetical to experimentation and risk-taking, let alone collaboration and transparency. What teacher wants to share a challenging instructional problem when everyone is operating under a magnifying glass? Standardization can discourage innovation and local adaptation.

An opposite approach is to treat teaching like a profession, which requires a graduate education in many states and a commitment to lifelong learning. This approach recognizes that teachers spend more time in the classroom and have more knowledge of conditions "on the ground" than anyone. In this case, teacher leadership has real meaning.

Here are two examples of teacher leaders who still lead with a spirit of social entrepreneurialism. Alicia Carroll is a teacher with fifteen years of experience in the classroom. She was a founding member of Mission Hill School, under the direction of the well-known Deborah Meier.[18] In recent years, she has addressed issues of race and culture through a curriculum project based on a book she wrote, called *Malindi's Journey*.[19] The book traces the journey of a giraffe from Africa to China and reenacts the historical trade connections between the two regions, thus reawakening urban school children to their own origins and expanding their minds to the greater world. Alicia collaborates with other educators in Africa, China, and the United States. Her kindergartners rebuild Malindi's boat in their own classroom. This curriculum is designed to provide a basis for cultural pride, even as she teaches history and geography to young students.

Jessie Auger is another example of a teacher leader with an innovative message.[20] She teaches first graders in a two-way Spanish/English bilingual school. Jessie works with other teachers in her school to design an integrated curriculum. She also offers workshops on mathematics and poetry across her city. What makes her unique is that she is also a member of a sister city project in San José Las Flores, El Salvador, where she travels often. This rural village has a long history of resisting political oppression and promoting free elections and public education. In her travels, Auger engages US and Salvadoran teachers in critical community dialogue. Back home, she raises money and connects students internationally through pen-pals.

Critics may question whether building a boat in a kindergarten classroom or connecting with teachers from El Salvador is the best way to boost student achievement. The argument is made, not unreasonably, that all children deserve access to the same curriculum everywhere and that teachers must deliver this curriculum faithfully. From this perspective, the best teacher leadership is compliant.

The organizational culture of public education has not been especially conducive to teacher leadership, and particularly an entrepreneurial brand of teacher leadership, since the administrative progressives gained precedence over the pedagogical progressives almost one hundred years ago.[21] The more Deweyan, democratic form of education has struggled to find a place in America. During this time period, there have been two major studies of the culture of teaching, which were separated by forty-three years; both found the orientation of the profession to be marked by conservatism, individualism, and presentism.[22] No doubt, the conservative, anti-entrepreneurial nature of the teaching profession has many causes, but the bureaucratic organizational culture of education must certainly be a top reason.

The factory model of education prevailed for over one hundred years in America, and the boxed classrooms, desks in rows, age-graded sorting of students, and standardized curriculum are all evidences. Doing the same thing that has been done in the past, with even more intensity, is not a sound approach to school reform. Hence, the argument for innovation in education and the need for entrepreneurial leadership. Innovation is needed in the classroom, day by day, to address the learning needs of students who come with diverse learning needs, languages, and backgrounds. Innovation is needed organizationally to uncover new structural and cultural approaches that are less restrictive and will unleash human talents.

The essence of entrepreneurial leadership is creative, experimental risk-taking in pursuit of a better idea. There is an artistry to this work which is now under threat in this country where, increasingly, the arts are being crowded out by other academic disciplines. Teacher leadership is not teacher compliance promoted as courageous leadership. True teacher leaders push the envelope, ask tough questions, challenge assumptions, and look for better ways to do things.

## HOW DO TEACHERS PERCEIVE TEACHER LEADERSHIP?

As the definition of teacher leadership has shifted over the years, so has the understanding of who gets to do the defining. Administrators tend to look for assistants who can assume some of their responsibilities, whereas teachers value other things when they think about teacher leadership. Two researchers decided to ask teachers, instead of administrators, to identify the teacher leaders in their school. They identified five possible categories of leadership—teacher as decision maker, educational role model, positional designee, supra-practitioner, and visionary—but the teachers were most likely to choose the educational role model as a teacher leader and least likely to choose the positional designee (the principal's appointment). From the teachers' point of view, the "exemplary teacher" was the real teacher leader.[23]

Teachers not only see teacher leadership differently, they are also skeptical about the shared model of leadership so often trumpeted by their principals.[24] For example, one research team reported that

> the responses of teachers in this study suggest that few changes have occurred in schools that are detectable by teachers. The groundswell of support for distributed conceptions of leadership may well be a kind of meta-rhetoric with little reality on the ground, reflecting a criticism often leveled at schools: that they are more concerned with the appearance of change than with the substance of change as a means of managing public legitimization of their work."[25]

In other words, teachers don't tend to agree with the administrative determination of teacher leadership, and they also don't agree that there is real support for teacher leadership. This is a serious indictment of the current organizational leadership of most schools.

When principals anoint some people as teacher leaders who are not recognized by their peers and fail to recognize others who are doing the real work of teacher leadership, they threaten administrative-staff collaboration and undermine the effectiveness of their faculty. Furthermore, when teacher leaders meet with their colleagues, but the principal dictates the agenda, they can further undermine the effectiveness of the PLCs.

Many teachers find ways to meet professionally, even on their own time, to address what they find important in school. Researchers call these independent groups communities of practice (COPs) to distinguish them from the more officially recognized PLCs.[26] In COPs, teachers are more likely to self-identify as teacher leaders and they are better able to determine the agenda.

PLCs are one administrative approach to distributing leadership in the school, which is not without benefit. When set up correctly, PLCs can be a means to empower teachers and engage them in planning, assessment, and instructional improvement. In contrast, COPs are a more grounded, grassroots approach to collaboration. They often go unnoticed.

The community of practice concept implies that each teacher assumes responsibility for personal and professional development. Rather than passively waiting for the school or district to determine where growth is needed and assign an appropriate workshop or coach, each teacher is a "learning entrepreneur" who identifies problems, visualizes solutions, finds resources, and assembles supportive teams as needed. [27] This self-directed approach to education is reminiscent of the ideas of Austrian philosopher and "maverick social critic" Ivan Ilich, [28] who challenged institutionalized systems of education in his radical book *Deschooling Society* in 1971 and called for networked learning webs instead. [29]

Being a learning entrepreneur is important for students as well as teachers. Too often, schooling is a passive affair, which leaves students disengaged and unmotivated. [30] Contrast this with teachers and students who own their learning and have some choices about what and how they will learn. Social learning theory predicts that students will learn the behaviors that are encouraged and modeled by their teachers. Teacher compliance will reproduce student apathy, while the teacher who is a learning entrepreneur is more likely to reproduce students who are also.

The attraction of the COP framework is that "COPs were originally conceived from an anthropological perspective with the aim of describing how newcomers are enculturated into a historically situated community with established traditions, roles, and practices." [31] In other words, the COP framework addresses teacher learning in the context of the larger school institution and considers how each affects the other. This is the ideal mechanism for the cultural reform strategy.

Teacher leadership is indispensable for the cultural reform strategy—and cultural reform strategy is central to creating an entrepreneurial organization. The school that is an entrepreneurial organization will be brimming with self-appointed teacher leaders. Rather than being a threat to administrative leadership, entrepreneurial teacher leaders—like all entrepreneurs—do not aspire to power or promotion, do not demand a lot of maintenance, and offer a level of energy, voluntarism, and creativity that will exceed any contract.

## STRATEGIES FOR EFFECTIVE ENTREPRENEURIAL COMMUNITIES OF PRACTICE

Communities of practice can be great, creative sources for new curriculum, instructional strategies, and even, as was demonstrated by the Academy of Public Service, new school programs. Creative work requires particular thinking strategies.[32] One of the oldest and most successful is brainstorming as first proposed by the creativity theorist Alex Osborn in 1957.[33] In groups, people are often fearful of offering novel ideas, so Osborn suggested that people meet first independently and write down their ideas, which are submitted anonymously. In the group, a facilitator reads and the group studies the feasibility of each suggestion.

Some scholars suggest that group members adopt particular roles for effective brainstorming. For example, the "client" might be a teacher who poses a classroom problem and sets up the schedule for brainstorming.[34] Other teachers would adopt a resource role with an attitude toward "how to" instead of "why not." One important member would always be the "passionate champion" who, after the group coalesces around a popular idea, leads everyone toward implementation.[35] When properly followed, these tactics can avoid groupthink and help move good ideas into action.

## PRINCIPALS WHO ENCOURAGE ENTREPRENEURIAL TEACHER LEADERSHIP

There is almost universal belief (except among teachers) that the school principal plays a crucial role in the emergence and development of teacher leadership. One book, for example, promoted the principal as "the key vehicle in advancing the cause of teacher leadership."[36]

Teacher leaders themselves, however, are less likely to point to the principal as the chief reason for their empowerment. For example, the entrepreneurial teacher leaders at Dunbar High School universally agreed that the school principals were *not* the reason for their emergence or effectiveness. In fact, some claimed that they exercised leadership *despite* the school principal.[37] In truth, principals might be more effective in preventing entrepreneurial teacher leadership than in promoting it.

In reality, "While generally supportive of the concept of teacher leadership, principals may lack the knowledge and experience required to effectively support higher levels of such leadership."[38] Principals simply may not know how to promote teacher leadership.

One thing principals can do to promote teacher entrepreneurism is to hire a diverse teaching force. A diverse faculty brings numerous benefits, such as cultural competence and role modeling with an equally diverse student body. However, there is more to a diverse faculty than just representation. Too often diversity is perceived superficially as a means to address internal discrimination or to better connect with constituents. This kind of thinking, however, pigeonholes diversity instead of championing the mix of new thinking that comes with a diverse teaching force. Staff members who represent different races, ethnicities, cultures, and histories bring diverse perspectives to school problems, which can open the doors to new solutions.[39]

Communities of practice that are diverse are better positioned for creativity and entrepreneurialism. Chapter 3 presented some organizational characteristics that are associated with innovative thinking, such as flattened hierarchies and integrative cultures. While a school organization might be struggling to be more integrative, a community of practice can enjoy the benefits of a more egalitarian culture where diverse perspectives are welcomed. The community of practice can become an island where transparency, openness to new ideas, and constructive conflict are welcome.

Another interesting principal approach to stimulating entrepreneurism, which comes from the world of business, is to "create vacuums rather than imposing solutions."[40] Experts encourage leaders to ask "what if" questions, which stir the imagination and invite creative, alternative solutions. This open-ended approach is very similar to the suggestions of Heifetz and Laurie (first presented in chapter 1) who distinguished between technical and adaptive problems.[41]

A related approach is seen when leaders carve out a particular problem for more attention and specify the constraints. When leaders specify the limits as well as the opportunities, followers are more likely to focus their imaginations to arrive at solutions.[42] This is not unlike the brainstorming strategy outlined earlier; the "client" raises a pointed question, which leads to independent brainstorming. The skillful principal who acts as a "client" must weigh the advantages of specifying constraints versus high-jacking the entire agenda and stifling other valuable innovations.

The history at Dunbar High points to another stimulus for teacher leadership, which is largely overlooked: community partnerships. For example, the three founders of APS were recruited by the Private Industry Council, indoctrinated through meetings with the American Society of Public Administrators, along with trips to Chicago and New

York, and then funded through philanthropies, such as the Trefler Foundation. Four principals came and went, while APS grew and matured.

The partners offered benefits that were not always present in the school, including recognition and an invitation to dream. Usually, they provided support, more often emotional and psychological than financial, although the partners could offer concrete items such as materials, transportation, or media promotion. Often, the partners linked teachers to other, new community partnerships, which expanded the resource base. This investment of confidence along with tangible resources was an important step in the emergence of teacher leadership. Furthermore, the partners provided room for risk-taking experimentation without threat of supervision, evaluation, and possible termination.

In some cases, the partners proved to be powerful advocates for the teacher leaders, when administrative forces, either locally or centrally, threatened to undo their accomplishments.[43] Chapter 6 looks more closely at the role of school partnerships.

## PARALLEL LEADERSHIP

New models of leadership, such as *parallel* leadership, offer a helpful model of how teachers and principals can freely exercise their leadership talents with less chance of stepping on one another's toes.[44] Rather than competing for leadership, school principals can assume responsibility for vision-casting, securing resources, and networking with community partners, while teachers exercise responsibility for classroom instruction. If it is true that teachers are often the chief source of entrepreneurism in schools, then parallel leadership would offer a way to unleash this innovative talent.

Smylie and Hart further clarified these parallel roles by distinguishing human from social capital.[45] Human capital is an individual construct, which measures value in terms of knowledge, skills, and dispositions. This is often connected to graduate degrees, licensure, or years of experience. In contrast, social capital measures the resources engendered through relationships. When teacher leaders collaborate and promote their colleagues, then social capital increases. When relationships are broken because teachers retire, move to another school, or are unable to meet together because of schedule changes, then social capital decreases.

School principals are encouraged to be instructional leaders in their building, but they also wrestle with their own limitations. While most began their career as teachers, they are well aware that they are not experts in all aspects of instructional pedagogy, let alone content, especially in the upper grades. In some cases, principals will call in outside experts who may lack contextual understanding.

Teachers are very aware of these limitations. One survey of 1,500 K–5 teachers in New York City found that "teachers were almost twice as likely to turn to their peers as to the experts designated by the school district, and four times more likely to seek advice from one another than from the principal."[46]

Principals can increase human capital by hiring better teachers, when the opportunity presents itself. (This is also an opportunity to address diversity, as described earlier.) However, most principals, especially at the high school level, struggle to improve individual human capital through professional development. On the other hand, they can facilitate relationships among teachers, knowing that teachers can learn from one another, which increases both social and human capital. They can line up mentors with new teachers and coaches for veteran teachers. Then can encourage PLCs and create schedules that provide free periods to groups of teachers so they can meet. School leaders are better at—and should concentrate on—developing social capital in their school rather than fixating on building human capital through professional development.

Social capital is important for teacher learning and the development of human capital. Social capital is also indispensable for entrepreneurism because of the opportunities for sharing ideas in a safe environment. It turns out that social capital is also important for student learning. One study of New York City math teachers found,

> Students showed higher gains in math achievement when their teachers reported frequent conversations with their peers that centered on math, and when there was a feeling of trust or closeness among teachers. In other words, teacher social capital was a significant predictor of student achievement gains above and beyond teacher experience or ability in the classroom.[47]

Equally important, teachers with *low* teaching ability but high social capital showed math gains equal to the *average* teachers in the school.[48]

This research raises questions about current turnaround school policy, which is directed at replacing up to half the teachers in underperforming schools. Obviously, this diminishes social capital. This might not be so bad if teacher networks have only reinforced old habits and low expectations for student learning. The conundrum is that teacher turnover also dismantles positive relationships. Teachers are reluctant to develop strong, trusting horizontal relationships when they know that a neighbor might be gone the next year. The damage to social capital could negatively impact teacher innovation and, ultimately, student achievement.

Carrie Leana, who led this research in New York City, also questioned the current emphasis on instructional leadership and looked at how principals spent their time during the day by tracking them with personal digital assistants. In an average work week of forty-nine hours, the principals spent twenty-eight hours on administrative matters, twelve hours on instructional leadership, such as monitoring or mentoring teachers, and only seven hours on external relations, including meetings with parents or community partners. However, it was this last activity that really made the difference for student achievement, while the instructional leadership activities had little impact. As she said,

> When principals spent more time building external social capital, the quality of instruction in the school was higher and students' scores on standardized tests in both reading and math were higher. Conversely, principals spending more of their time mentoring and monitoring teachers had no effect on teacher social capital or student achievement. The more effective principals were those who defined their roles as *facilitators* of teacher success rather than instructional leaders. They provided teachers with the resources they needed to build social capital—time, space, and staffing—to make the informal and formal connections possible. [49]

Parallel leadership allows principals and teachers to exercise leadership in their own domains. Teachers are free to build social capital in communities of practice, which provide a safe haven for posing problems and sharing ideas. This provides the setting for innovative approaches to instruction, which make for gains in student achievement. Parallel leadership promotes teacher entrepreneurism.

## CONCLUSION

This chapter presented teacher leadership as one aspect of leadership in an entrepreneurial school. Teacher leaders belie the belief that school principals are the only important leaders—and the only significant entrepreneurs. In fact, teacher leaders are often the innovative engines of the school.

The study of teacher leadership also helps to undo the "great man" theory of leadership, which places an undo emphasis on unique, heroic individuals. No doubt, there are rare cases of unique, go-it-alone leaders who bring about significant change. Jaime Escalante is one example of this Schumpeterian leader. Most leaders, however, are imitators, exploiters, opportunists—stealers, as Picasso says. Their ability to gain followers and willingness to take the classroom, or the school, in new directions is the proof of their leadership.

Furthermore, entrepreneurial leadership is not a go-it-alone experience. The Academy of Public Service teachers worked as a team. The Compact Ventures initiative of chapter 4 was a team effort. The early college program of chapter 2 was a team effort. In each case, entrepreneurial individuals shared ideas, raised important questions, learned from one another, and together crafted innovations for kids. They worked across boundaries with partners from outside the school.

Researchers are increasingly interested in this kind of collective behavior. Proximity and collaboration can increase innovative thinking. Are there other unseen advantages in collective behaviors and the development of social capital?[50]

Thomas W. Malone, founding director of the MIT Center for Collective Intelligence, said, "Intuitively, we still attribute too much to individuals and not enough to groups."[51] He and his team split 699 volunteers up into small groups of two to five members and gave them intelligence challenges, such as guessing the next item in a sequence or brainstorming innovative uses for a brick. In this way, they were able to measure the *collective* intelligence of the group. They quickly discovered that *collective* intelligence did not correlate with the *average* intelligence of the group members. Furthermore, *collective* intelligence could not be predicted by looking at the group member with the highest IQ. In other words, *collective* intelligence was based on factors other than individual IQ.

Malone and his team looked for other explanations of collective success, such as the group's motivation or satisfaction or the cohesiveness of the group, but all proved irrelevant. They did find three predictors, however. First, members who were good at reading one another's emotions boosted collective intelligence. Secondly, and perhaps related, as the ratio of women in a group increased, the collective intelligence did also. And finally, groups with a dominant member who monopolized the conversation tended to have low collective intelligence.[52]

Malone and his team admit that they have barely scratched the surface when it comes to understanding collective intelligence. However, they are joined by others, in many fields, who are seeking to understand this hidden social phenomenon. Reports now indicate that "new knowledge is increasingly being produced by teams."[53] This is where innovation happens. This is why social capital is indispensable for the creative work of good teaching.

The implications for schooling are startling. Individual IQ is considered fixed (although there are many who challenge this assumption). However, the early research on collective intelligence suggests that this social phenomenon is malleable. Groups of students, as well as teachers, can gain intelligence as they learn to work together. Their collective intelligence will outstrip any one member of the group.

In an ideal world, students will be lifelong learners, which means that their teachers must be also. Public schooling is not just a technical problem that can be addressed with sufficient textbooks and a scripted curriculum. Education is an adaptive problem, which means the people who own the problem—the teachers—must brainstorm the solutions, take risks, and learn from their mistakes.[54] The school must be nothing less than a learning organization.[55]

All this calls for entrepreneurial teachers. Good teachers are dedicated to innovative ideas, not just those that are handed to them from the nation's capital or the superintendent's office, but those that are designed from the bottom up in the context where they work. Teacher leaders are the heart of the entrepreneurial schoolhouse.

## NOTES

1. This list of traits is gleaned from Harris, A. (2005). Teacher leadership: More than just a feel-good factor? *Leadership and Policy in Schools, 4*(3), 201–219; Hilty, E. B. (Ed.). (2011). *Teacher leadership: The 'new' foundations of teacher education.* New York: Peter Lang; Murphy, J. (2005). *Connecting teacher leadership and school improvement.* Thousand Oaks, CA: Corwin Press; Wynne, J. (2001). *Teachers as leaders in education reform. ERIC Digest.* Washington, DC: Eric Clearinghouse on Teaching and Teacher Education.

2. Angelle, P. S., & Schmid, J. B. (2007). School structure and the identity of teacher leaders: Perspectives of principals and teachers. *Journal of School Leadership, 17*(6), 771–799.

3. Northouse, P. G. (2010). *Leadership: Theory and practice* (5th ed.). Washington, DC: Sage.

4. York-Barr, J., & Duke, K. (2004). What do we know about teacher leadership? Findings from two decades of scholarship. *Review of Educational Research, 74*(3), 288.

5. Angelle, P. S., & Schmid, J. B., 775.

6. Norton, J. (2010, February 24). Creating young teacher leaders, para. 15. *Teacher Magazine.* Retrieved from http://www.edweek.org/tm/articles/2010/02/24/tln_norton_teacherleadership.html?r=1456806539.

7. Acker-Hocevar & Touchton, 1999, p. 26, as cited in York-Barr, J., & Duke, K., 265.

8. York-Barr, J., & Duke, K., 287–88.

9. This case study is taken from Gonsalves, L., & Leonard, J. (2007). *New hope for urban high schools: Cultural reform, moral leadership and community partnership*. Westport, CT: Praeger; Leonard, J. (2002). History of a high school community, 1950–2000 (Massachusetts). *DAI, 63*(02A), 318.

10. Shear, L., Means, B., Mitchell, K., House, A., Gorges, T., Joshi, A., et al. (2008). Contrasting paths to small-school reform: Results of a 5-year evaluation of the Bill & Melinda Gates Foundation's National High Schools Initiative. *Teachers College Record, 110*(9), 1986–2039.

11. Menendez, R. (Writer) & Musca, T. (Producer). (1988). *Stand and deliver*. [motion picture]. United States, Warner Bros.

12. Rogers, C. (1995). *On becoming a person: A therapist's view of psychotherapy*. Boston, MA: Mariner Books.

13. Guggenheim, D. (Writer) & Chilcott, L. (Producer). (2010). *Waiting for "Superman."* [motion picture]. United States, Paramount Vantage.

14. Scholars summarize the evolution in various ways. See, for example, Harris, A., Murphy, J., Silva, D. Y., Gimbert, B., & Nolan, J. (2000). Sliding the doors: Locking and unlocking possibilities for teacher leadership. *Teachers College Record, 102*(4), 779–804.

15. Murphy, J.

16. DuFour, R., & Eaker, R. (1998). *Professional learning communities at work: Best practices for enhancing student achievement*. Bloomington, IN: Solution Tree.

17. Harris, A. (2003). Teacher leadership as distributed leadership: Heresy, fantasy or possibility? *School Leadership & Management, 23*(3), 9.

18. Mission Hill K–8 School. (2013). Retrieved March 9, 2013, from http://www.missionhillschool.org/.

19. Carroll, A. (2010). Malindi's journey. Retrieved March 7, 2013, from http://malindisjourney.blogspot.com/.

20. Driscoll, D. P. (2006). 2007 Massachusetts teacher of the year brochure. Retrieved March 9, 2013, from http://www.doe.mass.edu/educators/recognition/toy/07broch.html.

21. Urban, W. J., & Wagoner, J. L., Jr. (2009). *American education: A history*. New York: Routledge.

22. Lortie, D. C. (1975). *Schoolteacher: A sociological study*. Chicago: University of Chicago Press; Waller, W. (1961). *Sociology of teaching*. New York: Russell and Russell. Waller's book was first published in 1932.

23. Angelle, P. S., & Schmid, J. B., 784–85.

24. York-Barr, J., & Duke, K.

25. Leithwood, K., & Mascall, B. (2008). Collective leadership effects on student achievement. *Educational Administration Quarterly, 44*(4), 550.

26. Santamaria, L., & Thousand, J. (2004). Collaboration, co-teaching, and differentiated instruction: A process-oriented approach to whole schooling. *International Journal of Whole Schooling, 1*(1), 13–27.

27. The term "learning entrepreneur" was coined by K. Olson (2011, March 1). If you were a learning entrepreneur. *Education Week Teacher*.

28. Madar, C. (2010). The people's priest. *The American Conservative*, para. 1. Retrieved from http://www.theamericanconservative.com/articles/the-peoples-priest/.

29. Illich, I. (2000). *Deschooling society*. London: Marion Boyars Publishers Ltd.

30. Steinberg, L., Brown, B. B., & Dornbusch, S. M. (1996). *Beyond the classroom: Why school reform has failed and what parents need to do*. New York: Simon and Schuster.

31. Butler, D. L., Lauscher, H. N., Jarvis-Selinger, S., & Beckingham, B. (2004). Collaboration and self-regulation in teachers' professional development. *Teaching & Teacher Education: An International Journal of Research and Studies, 20*(5), 437.

32. Amabile, T. M. (1997). Motivating creativity in organizations: On doing what you love and loving what you do. *California Management Review, 40*(1), 39–58; Amabile, T. M. (1998). How to kill creativity. *Harvard Business Review, 76*(5), 76–87.

33. Adams, K. (2005). *The sources of innovation and creativity* (p. 59). Washington, DC: National Center on Education and the Economy.

34. Govindarajan, V., & Terwilliger, J. (2012, July 25). Yes, you can brainstorm without groupthink, para. 7. Retrieved from http://blogs.hbr.org/cs/2012/07/yes_you_can_brainstorm_without.html.

35. Govindarajan, V., & Terwilliger, J., para. 10.

36. Crowther, F., Kaagan, S. S., Ferguson, M., & Hann, L. (2002). *Developing teacher leaders: How teacher leadership enhances school success*. Thousand Oaks, CA: Corwin Press, 77.

37. Leonard, J.

38. York-Barr, J., & Duke, K., 274.

39. Thomas, D. A., & Ely, R. J. (1996). Making differences matter: A new paradigm for managing diversity. *Harvard Business Review, 74*(5), 79–90.

40. Kelly, J., & Nadler, S. (2007). Leading from below. *MIT Sloan Management Review, 46*(3), para. 37. Retrieved from http://sloanreview.mit.edu/executive-adviser/2007-1/4917/leading-from-below/.

41. Heifetz, R. A., & Laurie, D. L. (1997). The work of leadership. *Harvard Business Review, 75*(1), 124–134.

42. Gupta, V., MacMillan, I. C., & Surie, G. (2004). Entrepreneurial leadership: Developing and measuring a cross-cultural construct. *Journal of Business Venturing, 19*(2), 241–260.

43. Gonsalves, L., & Leonard, J.

44. Andrews, D., & Crowther, F. (2002). Parallel leadership: A clue to the contents of the "black box" of school reform. *International Journal of Educational Management, 16*(4), 152–159.

45. Smylie, M. A., & Hart, A. W. (2000). School leadership for teacher learning and change: A human and social capital development perspective. In

J. Murphy & K. S. Louis (Eds.), *Handbook of research on educational administration* (2nd ed., pp. 421–441). San Francisco: Jossey-Bass.

46. Leana, C. R. (2011). The missing link in school reform. *Stanford Social Innovation Review, 9*(4), 33.

47. Leana, C. R., 33.

48. Leana, C. R., 34.

49. Leana, C. R., 35. Carrie Leana, who led this research, is an interesting example of thinking outside the box. She holds appointments in the Graduate School of Business, the Graduate School of Public and International Affairs, and the School of Medicine at the University of Pittsburgh—but not the school of education. To read her work is a boundary-crossing experience and is a great example of what can happen when we allow ourselves to learn from other disciplines.

50. Surowiecki, J. (2005). *The wisdom of crowds: Why the many are smarter than the few and how collective wisdom shapes business, economies, societies and nations.* New York: Anchor.

51. Johnson, C. Y. (2010, December 19). Group IQ. *The Boston Globe,* para. 5. Retrieved from http://www.boston.com/bostonglobe/ideas/articles/2010/12/19/group_iq/.

52. Johnson, C. Y.

53. Johnson, C. Y., para. 16.

54. Heifetz, R. A., & Laurie, D. L. (1997). The work of leadership. *Harvard Business Review, 75*(1), 124–134; Heifetz, R. A., & Linsky, M. (2002). *Leadership on the line: Staying alive through the dangers of leading.* Boston: Harvard Business School Press.

55. Senge, P. (2006). *The fifth dimension: The art and practice of the learning organization.* New York: Doubleday.

# 6

# PARTNERSHIPS FOR ENTREPRENEURIAL INNOVATION

There are frequent calls for out-of-the-box thinking in education, and sometimes this requires literally getting out of the brick-and-mortar school building. The heavy demands of urban education can tie the school administrator or the teacher to the school setting, but partnering with community businesses, colleges, and social service agencies can lead to innovative breakthroughs.

Researchers examined the up-and-down fortunes of one inner city high school and discovered the powerful impact of community partners working in collaboration with small teams of teachers from the school. Chapter 6 of this book is devoted to this partnering work. Bronfenbrenner's ecological systems theory sheds light on how skillful partnering can generate new ideas and improve learning outcomes for students. The use of school partnerships is a proven strategy for entrepreneurial innovation, but one that is often overlooked and also filled with pitfalls.

## THE POWER AND PROMISE OF PARTNERSHIPS IN EDUCATION

Everyone has an idea of school partnerships, but the concept is surprisingly difficult to define. Usually, one thinks of organizations in the community, such as local businesses or the nearby university. However, partners can also include the neighborhood health center, a social service agency, or an office for housing or employment. There is also a nationwide movement of community schools, sometimes called full-

service schools; these schools deliberately link the classroom with
health and social services for comprehensive care for the whole family.[1]
Some schools partner with faith-based organizations, philanthropies for
fundraising and networking, various industries for job placement, or
even other schools in order to share resources or create a more coher-
ent pipeline for children. The list is endless.

Parents, of course, are the most important members of the outside-
the-school community and are often included in discussions of partnerships.[2] They are addressed only obliquely in this chapter for two reasons. First, there is ample literature on parental engagement, and, secondly, parents are not a typical driver for innovation. This chapter focuses on the role of partnering for entrepreneurial leadership.

Partnerships come in many shapes and sizes as well. Consider just
one category, for example—partnerships between schools and universities—and one finds that there are agreements that provide new teacher training and mentoring, professional development for veteran teachers, curriculum development, consulting services, research services,
dual-enrollment courses, precollegiate activities for youth, and a combination of all this and more.[3] In other words, each partnership can in-
volve a single or multiple points of engagement.

Finally, every school is tied to a variety of outside agencies that
might not normally be considered partners, such as the superintendent's office, other schools in the district K–12 sequence, the local
police and fire departments, inspectional services, state and federal
governments, and even the local media. These arrangements are often
obligatory, but they could be nudged in a voluntary direction to support
activities such as guest speakers and career exploration, internships,
donations to the yearbook, and so on.

Partnerships imply mutuality and collaboration. For example,
schools in partnership with universities cannot just be the passive recip-
ients of the latter's high-minded scholastic expertise. Instead, K–12
schools have their own expertise gained through daily, on-the-ground
experience, which is essential for teacher preparation programs and
engaged forms of scholarship. Knowledge flows both ways.[4]

A useful definition for education partnerships is "institutions working together with mutual respect, sustained commitment, agreed-upon
benefits for all partners, interdependence, engagement of all stakeholders, and trust."[5] The emphasis on mutuality, commitment, respect, and
trust makes clear that some obligatory relationships do not always qualify as partnerships.

There are many directions to explore with school partnerships, since
this is a huge field. After a brief disclaimer about business partnerships,
this chapter uses two theories to help understand a complex case study

about a school-community partnership and then concludes with some how-to advice and some imagination-tickling depictions of large-scale, big-city partnerships that are getting great results for children.

## CAVEATS AND CONCERNS

First, school-community partnerships are not a silver-bullet solution for the problems of public education. Partnerships take time and a lot of attention, as this chapter will demonstrate. They exact "transaction costs," which include a lot of valuable time devoted to finding the partnership, developing relationships of trust and mutual respect, and then nursing the partnership over time.[6] Getting everyone to the table is a challenge everyone recognizes. Once together, there are cultural clashes, differing agendas, and miscommunications.[7] Of course, this is true of all relationships, whether internal communities of practice or external school partnerships, but the potential benefits of collaboration outweigh the risks.

A second concern has to do with business partnerships. The topic of school partnerships, particularly with large corporations, is complicated, since partnerships can be an open door for commercialization, exploitation, and subversion of the democratic purposes of education. One scholar, for example, studied the competitive world of school fundraising in Canada and raised numerous "equity and ethical concerns" about this uneven and episodic funding strategy.[8] Some schools prospered more than others; some schools were open to overt branding. Furthermore the fundraising relieved pressure on the government to provide proper funding.

The purpose of this book is not to turn the schools over to big-business corporations. Quite the opposite; the goal is to steal (Picasso-style) the best of what business has to offer, while still honoring the principles of mutuality, commitment, respect, and trust defined earlier. Businesses are amazing sources of innovation; they have much to teach about entrepreneurial leadership and they can bring valuable resources and expertise to public education.

Entrepreneurial educators are pragmatists who are driven primarily by the question, "What works for my students?" When Ralph Spezio wanted to build a preschool alongside his urban elementary school, he didn't quibble about the profit-making motive of the building contractor who donated materials. He was a resource scavenger. Thus, he ended up with a historically important preschool. Lynn Gatto and Alicia Carroll (chapter 5), both entrepreneurial teachers, worked closely with publishing companies to develop curriculum that would benefit their children.

One of the small learning communities at Dunbar High School was a business academy, which became an independent school in the final round of restructuring in 2003. The business-themed inner city school was closely allied with the TJX Companies. To their credit, TJX provided a host of services with little tangible payback. Each year, they funded a September field day, which acclimated nervous ninth graders to the school and melded them into a team. They bused sophomores, juniors, and seniors out to company headquarters where thirty to forty staff members gave up their day to run hands-on workshops on marketing, merchandising, and job interview skills. Guest speakers came to the school and offered leadership classes. Each year, they donated $10,000 in college scholarships, plus school bags, calculators, pens, pencils, and other classroom materials.

The school sent teachers and administrators to meet with company executives every summer to plan the year's activities. This day of creative brainstorming birthed the innovations described previously, which were field-tested at the business academy and often duplicated in other schools across the country. TJX groomed their community spirit image at this school. No doubt, the students grew to love the TJX brand, but these were low-income inner city students, hardly big spenders.

Is there a place for corporate donations in funding public education? No doubt. The president of *Funding Education Partners*, an organization "committed to use the power of business to solve social problems,"[9] despaired of the erosion of taxpayer-provided education funds. He saw a place for branding in schools, which could be lucrative for both partners:

> Make no mistake, these are for-profit companies that partner with schools while seeking to drive revenue, improve margins, and create shareholder value, all the while leveraging parents as an extension of their sales teams and students as their "feet on the street." It's time for a new model. It's time to recognize the reality of our long-term education funding crisis and welcome credible Fortune 500 companies into public schools.[10]

The business academy was an under-resourced urban school where students were painfully aware of the sub-standard facilities compared to their suburban peers. There was no swimming pool, theater, or stadium. The 1980s windows had long since frosted over, the brick walls leaked during rainstorms, the track team practiced in the hallways, and the auditorium lacked proper lighting. In partnering with TJX, the school was simply playing catch-up. Such is the case with many urban and rural schools in America. The partnership worked well for students who were eager to learn all they could about business.

In reality, the community is already on the doorstep and well inside the local school. In the past fifty years, schools have seen a steady onslaught of new laws, standards, and reporting requirements that have invited legal advocates, law enforcement officers, publishers, and politicians into the schools. Not a day goes by where school leaders do not deal with community groups, venders, the media, and a host of other outsiders. The public schools desperately need allies.

Michael Fullan, a well-known Canadian scholar on school reform, took a positive approach to all this. He wrote,

> The "out there" has now moved "in here." Forces that previously were outside are now in teachers' faces every day. The first lesson of the inside-out story is counterintuitive: most outside forces that have moved inside threaten schools in some way, but they are also necessary for success . . . In light of this new reality, teachers and principals must reframe their roles and shift their orientations to the outside.[11]

In other words, Fullan believed that the community posed a threat, but could also offer an opportunity. This ability to find opportunity where others perceive risk is in itself very entrepreneurial.

Positive leadership for school reform can come from many directions, including community partners. Sometimes, the real story of school reform is larger than the local school, larger than the principal. The history at Dunbar revealed many committed partnering leaders at the university, among the businesses, and in central administration.[12]

Our schools cannot and *should not* singlehandedly tackle the job of educating the nation's children, even if ample government support were available. The history of the community school movement underscores the importance of wrap-around services that support the intellectual, physical, social, and psychological development of our children. The development of the next generation is too important to relegate to one set of professionals. If ever there is a place where "it takes a village," public education is that place. Education is a national concern with social, civic, political, intellectual, and economic consequences, which have relevance to every American. This chapter is a plea for educational leaders at every level to forcefully and persistently promote the moral necessity of public engagement by all possible partners, including big business.

## TWO THEORIES

There are two theories of organization that contribute to an under-standing of school-community partnerships and how to use them to spark educational improvements. One theory takes an expansive view of all the partnering activity, while the second theory of tight and loose coupling directs our attention to the individual links. [13]

Ecological systems theory draws attention to the entire environment of the developing school child and the adaptive fit of the child to that environment. There are various ways to depict this relationship. Joyce Epstein, for example, is an ecological systems person who has written extensively on the benefits of close parent-school communication and collaboration. [14] Her work features a triangle that links the school, fami-ly, and community around the developing child.

Urie Bronfenbrenner greatly developed ecological systems theory. He proposed that the developing child is surrounded by layers of rela-tionships like a set of nested Russian dolls. [15] The inner circle, which he called the microsystem, described those settings in which the child had direct, face-to-face relationships with parents, friends, or teachers. Or-dinarily, there are cross-relationships between these small settings—parents talk to teachers, for example—and these lateral connections were called the mesosystem. Beyond this was an outer circle of people who were indirectly involved in the child's development, such as em-ployers, family health care workers, or central school administrators; this was called the exosystem. Businesses, universities, or social service agencies that partnered with the child's school would ordinarily be part of the exosystem. [16]

Bronfenbrenner explained that student development happened in the microsystems, where students lived every day. For this reason, par-ents, peers, and teachers had the maximum impact on student growth and everyone else—such as the parents' workplace, local church, health care agencies, and school-community partners, who were members of the exosystem—had an indirect effect, which was mediated through the microsystem partners.

Partners in the exosystem could maximize their impact on student development by moving toward the microsystem. This was a frequent strategy in the history of Dunbar's partners. For example, the Private Industry Council signed the Boston Compact with the public school system, but this citywide agreement created not a ripple at Dunbar High School until the PIC placed a career specialist inside the building. This person worked one-on-one with students to write résumés and develop interview skills; he joined the microsystem. He worked closely with teachers to make sure students were keeping their grades up and with outside employers to find available jobs. Suddenly, the PIC was providing jobs and boosting academic performance.

As another example, Pam Trefler was president of the Trefler Foundation in the 1990s and generously supported the Academy of Public Service (described more fully in chapter 5). However, Pam didn't just sit on the advisory board or donate money for others to spend. She came in every Monday and served as a teaching assistant in a ninth grade English classroom (a familiar place, since she had once been a student teacher at Dunbar). She volunteered to mentor some of the APS girls, which meant more than just sharing her business acumen, but also fielding late-night phone calls and helping find dresses for the spring prom. As a result, the impact of her foundation was felt locally.

A lot of movement toward school improvement happened at this local level, in these "pockets of excellence" where community partners moved in close to work with students and staff at the microsystem level.[17] These were tiny, interorganizational units, which had their own culture and connectedness. In some years, there were multiple places in the school where true reform was occurring, independently. Pam had a big impact on APS, for she met with this group frequently, but her visits were often unnoticed by other teams in the building.

Microsystems are small in nature. The PIC coordinator, Pam Trefler, and others demonstrated that it was equally important to coordinate with other adults at the microsystem level. Bronfenbrenner called these horizontal links the mesosystem. Wick's theory of organizational coupling, which was first presented in chapter 3, sheds some light on these connections.

Public schools are often described as loosely coupled organizations, which is a description of how information actually moves across the institution.[18] For example, school administrators are sometimes baffled that centrally mandated curriculum is not faithfully implemented, but rather re-interpreted in each classroom so that the end result bears little relationship to the original intention. The common saying is that "a lot is lost in the translation."

In the Academy of Public Service, the core teachers met every day as a community of practice to examine the needs of students and brainstorm strategies for success. Pam Trefler joined this group often, as did the PIC career specialist. As a result, there was tight coordination in program design in APS. Students heard the same message from all the significant adults at school.

When partners become part of the students' microsystem and begin to work intensively with other adults, as Pam did with the English teacher and the leaders of APS, the couplings are tightened. The partnership, this small "pocket of excellence," becomes a tightly coupled organization, which is operating inside a larger, loosely coupled institution. Under these conditions, significant educational innovations, which are appropriate for the targeted students, are more likely to be generated continually in a timely fashion.[19]

APS was loosely coupled to the larger school, which allowed it to retain its identity and adaptability. Loose coupling facilitates adaptability, which is the seedbed for innovation. Each pocket of excellence was able to respond to environmental challenges with agility and flexibility. As team members met new challenges, they were free to innovate. Creativity, experimentation, and risk-taking were exercised without fear. APS activities went "under the radar" in that they were largely unnoticed by school administrators, but internally, APS was a tightly coupled organization where innovations were implemented immediately, continually, and faithfully.

## MULTIPLE PARTNERS: EXOSYSTEM WORK

Pam was a fixture in the Academy of Public Service. Her personal presence increased her impact but also informed the foundation about the realities of school change for the entire city. In the late 1990s the foundation gave $1 million to fund a five-year, three-way partnership between the high school, the university, and her foundation. This partnership reflected the lessons learned at APS, including the value of personalized small learning communities, daily communities of practice, tight local coupling in a loosely coupled school, drilling down to the microsystem, and networking across the mesosystem. Within five years, the entire school was restructured into APS-like small learning communities. Subsequent gifts carried the strategies to other city high schools.[20]

Bronfenbrenner's depiction of the ecological system was complex, reflected in many propositions and hypotheses published in his seminal work. For example, he hypothesized that students' development in school would increase as the *number* of supportive partnering organizations increased.[21] Certainly, the late 1990s was a busy time at Dunbar High School. Trefler's large gift increased engagement with the foundation, the PIC, and the University of Massachusetts Boston. The university partnership was complex, with multiple points of contact, including a new full-time teacher preparation program, executive coaching, and researchers inserted into the school. They, in turn, brought other partners on board, including the Northeast and Islands Regional Education Laboratory and the Institute for Student Achievement.[22] Lesser partners included the neighborhood health center, an after-school program for teen empowerment, and several businesses.

Trefler's investment was not in vain. Dunbar's graduation rate, which was only 27 percent in the 1980s, grew to 41 percent by the late 1990s when the high school was being transformed into small learning communities. The average daily attendance, which dropped to 76 percent in the violence of the early 1990s, improved to 80 percent by 2000. More students were staying to graduate even though the work was harder. In 1985 students could graduate from DHS with only one general math course; by 1998, they were required to take four math courses and pass Advanced Algebra.[23] The new high-stakes state graduation exam meant they also had to be able to read and write. All this happened in an under-resourced school where over 90 percent of the students came from low-income families and 50 percent of the students were English language learners and/or students with disabilities. The community partners were undoubtedly a significant part of the gradual progress.

## CULTURAL COHESION

Chapter 4 introduced cultural reform theory as an important component of school turnaround work, alongside curricular and structural changes. When leaders pay attention to building healthy relationships, whether among students, student peers, teachers, parents, or community partners, they are employing a cultural reform strategy. Reculturalization is important if teachers, students, and administrators are going to own and implement new educational innovations.[24] However, cultural consistency is also necessary.

An increase in partners can often be a recipe for disaster, leading to an incoherent vision, reform efforts with conflicting purposes, and staff exhaustion.[25] Teachers and students can feel like they are pulled in different directions, raising anxiety levels and lowering trust. Just as parenting works better when both adults convey the same message to the child, so complementary messages across the microsystems are important for healthy student development.

Ecological systems theory offers important lessons for the coordination of partnerships. The degree of synergy or agreement among relationships—or "cultural cohesion"—is important for student development.[26] Bronfenbrenner also saw the constant need for cultural cohesion, which would be demonstrated by "the growth of mutual trust, positive orientation, goal consensus between settings and an evolving balance of power."[27] The history of Dunbar High School proved that this was not always the case.

## A BAD EXAMPLE

In some cases, community partners were affiliated with the school, but there was little coordination at the mesosystem level. The Institute for Student Achievement (ISA) placed two full-time teachers in the school who worked intensively with sixty students for four years, in school and after school, to prepare them for college.[28] They had a designated space within the building that was a second home for these students. The ISA was firmly established at the microsystem level. However, the ISA employees rarely interacted with the rest of the school faculty, so the students received mixed messages as they shuttled back and forth. ISA teachers promoted different schedules, priorities, and goals than the Dunbar teachers. The Dunbar teachers were suspicious and sometimes critical of the ISA agenda. There was no cultural cohesion. After four years, many of the students had transferred or dropped out and the college placement rate was unremarkable despite an enormous investment.[29] This was a failure among committed partners who did not achieve cultural cohesion.

## GOOD EXAMPLES

Dunbar High School was subdivided in 2003, and one of the new small schools determined to build a consistent message around a culture of achievement. The goal was that academics would be the conversation among students, teachers, parents, and partners. Students would not be embarrassed to talk about school, teachers would discuss their practice instead of their retirement, and parents would know more about academics than sports. The school took students on college tours in their freshmen year, taught them how to calculate their grade point average, and demonstrated that a few years of academic neglect would be hard to overcome later. Teachers who had constructive classroom strategies were promoted and encouraged to share with their peers.

The community partners were equally engaged to make sure that academics were foremost. One valuable partner focused on student leadership and they began to train students to lobby against the state high-stakes graduation exam (the Massachusetts Comprehensive Assessment System). The school principal intervened, however, and reasoned, "Our students have to pass this test to get a high school diploma. We can't afford to undermine their determination. When they graduate and go to college, they can major in political science and take up this battle." The partner readily agreed, and, together, they began to focus on other, more complementary leadership messages.

The school slowly developed this culture of achievement with the help of the community partners. The partners were the source of many entrepreneurial innovations. For example, the university partner worked with the school to create a summer orientation for eighth graders who were assigned to the high school, so they would feel at home on the first day of school. Their summer program included college readiness experiences on the university campus, tutoring in literacy and math as well as some great excursions around the city. Later, when students went out on business internships with the banking partner, the officers made sure there was always an academic component, such as presenting a report on their experience to their co-workers. And the Private Industry Council invented *Classroom at the Workplace,* a summer jobs program where students received two hours of math and English support at the start of the day.[30]

## TIGHT COUPLING ON A LARGER SCALE

Student impact is maximized when partners move toward the microsystem and begin to interact, but something else happens in this arena as well. Entrepreneurial leadership thrives in this context. Creativity ignites and innovations emerge. Trefler's large donation brought university professors into the high school every day for five years, where they interacted with students, teachers, and administrators. Numerous innovations came out of these face-to-face interactions. The Academy of Public Service was replicated across the school so that, within five years, every student at Dunbar was enjoying the advantages of a small learning community. Dunbar started its own, in-house alternative academy, with a competency-based curriculum, for students who did not succeed in the traditional classroom.[31]

At every stage, the partners asked the teachers, "What do you need?" and the teachers directed the ideas and resources toward the students. In one meeting, the teachers said, "We need more adults; we want to increase the teacher/student ratio." Working together, Trefler, the university, and Dunbar teachers created *Teach Next Year,* which was a full-time, year-long internship for aspiring teachers, which provided a master's degree and state licensure at the end of fifteen months.[32] This program gained national recognition and was later replicated by the Boston Public Schools.[33] *TNY* graduates were guaranteed a job in this school district, for they came with a solid year of first-hand urban experience under their belt. Dunbar hired as many as possible. These graduates often went on to become teacher leaders in ensuing years.[34] These creations were the result of intense work in the mesosystem.

Partners move toward the microsystem, as Trefler did when she taught in the APS English classroom, when they want to have maximum impact on student development. Sometimes, however, partners will work together across the exosystem because they want to maximize their impact on organizational change. In the late 1990s the Trefler Foundation began to collaborate with the PIC and the superintendent's office to bring about major change across the district.


## SUSTAINABILITY

One of the downsides of community partnerships is that they can be temporary. In many cases, the partnership is launched under the terms of some grant, and when the money runs out, the partnership disappears. Many grant funders attempt to address the problem of sustainability by requiring "capacity-building" as a goal of the partnership, which turns out to be more complicated than imagined.

Capacity-building can sometimes be interpreted as a one-way transfer of knowledge and expertise, which does not accurately reflect the mutuality, respect, and trust described earlier. For this reason, the goal of capacity-building can be insulting to a school since it implies a starting point of incapacity. Chapter 4 described a cohort of teachers who began working at Dunbar High School in the late 1960s called the "class of '69." Thanks to the New England Telephone Company, they received some T-training in the 1970s, a popular approach to team-building and goal-setting at that time, so their capacity was presumably increased. However, most of what this group learned they learned through years of experience. They spearheaded numerous innovations in the 1980s, including Compact Ventures and the Academy of Public Service.

A larger and related problem is that capacity cannot always be dispensed and deposited, like money in a bank.[35] Just as a basketball team develops a winning capacity as they practice together and learn to anticipate one another's movements, so a lot of the capacity of school partnerships lies within the relationships that are developed.[36] Members begin to trust one another, open up, share dreams, and take risks when they feel safe. When the relationships are broken off, the capacity vanishes.

For these reasons, school leaders must work for sustained partnerships that extend beyond the terms of the grant. This means that the issue of sustainability must be put on the table early in the relationship, much like a marriage contract. Developing trust is difficult under any other arrangement.

What does commitment look like? First, committed partners often have more than one point of contact. In other words, they find multiple ways to work together, as if each activity were another thread in the binding rope. In this way, more people from both institutions are drawn into partnership, find benefit, and will resist the decline of the partnership.[37]

Secondly, while the actual work of partnering is typically carried out by people in the middle of the organizational structure—such as the high school teachers and the PIC career specialist at Dunbar—it is imperative that there is visible support from the highest levels of each institution.[38] Pam Trefler was president of her foundation, and she attended many of the meetings herself. As another example, during the creation of the early college program (described in chapter 2), planning meetings were regularly attended by top-level administrators from both institutions: the college vice president of academics as well as the district superintendent and high school principal. When these people stopped attending, trust was undermined.

Another real sign of commitment is "real estate." Several scholars have pointed out that the addition of a designated office space with a sign and a telephone is an even better indicator of seriousness and sustainability.[39] This space could be reserved within either institution, or both.

## BOUNDARY SPANNERS

Every strong partnership needs a boundary spanner.[40] The boundary spanner is a person with feet planted in two organizations. The Dunbar High School partnership with the University of Massachusetts Boston depended on a person who was paid by the university but had an office at the school. Often called the *partnership coordinator* or *university liaison*, her job was to coordinate all the activities of the partnership, which meant that she worked every day with individuals from both schools. The work of boundary spanners is often described as *brokering*[41] when they negotiate and facilitate the flow of information and resources across the boundary and as *buffering* when they stand up to protect institutional interests on one end or the other. [42]

Boundary spanners come in all shapes and sizes. Some excel at the *spanning* work because they have outstanding people skills. They are natural networkers and enjoy putting people together. They are often fluent linguists and find no difficulty in speaking the language of two different institutional cultures. They perform valuable work in translating meaning and intention across the organizational boundary.

Other boundary spanners excel because they thrive on the edge. These people are like pioneers or scouts; they are restless in traditional settings and enjoy roaming the frontier. Often, their work is more exploratory, looking for new ways to connect the institutions. They are also good at discovering new partnerships.

Both kinds of boundary spanners tend to be entrepreneurial because they are good at breaking down associative barriers. [43] The human brain tends to categorize information in order to make sense of the world and to better retain important ideas. Each concept is developed mentally with a set of associations, which provide meaning but also delimit the imagination. Boundary spanners jump these constructs, and, rather than limit their thinking to predetermined categories, they excel at juxtaposing information from multiple sources and domains. This is a proven strategy for innovative thinking. [44]

In most partnerships, someone volunteers or is appointed to do the boundary-spanning work. In the early college planning program described in chapter 2, one of the college deans was a born boundary spanner. The dean reminded participants of the meetings, came with a prepared agenda, facilitated the discussions, pressed for decisions, and made sure plans were in place for the next meeting. She was not paid anything extra for this coordination work. Like many entrepreneurs, she tired of the project once it was established and required more management than leadership.

Without a boundary spanner, partnering work is often filled with miscommunication and mishaps. The *institutionalization* of a partnership almost requires an appointed boundary spanner. Schools and partners are more likely to seek this level of sustainability when they share a fundamental conviction that the education of the next generation is not the responsibility of schools alone.

## BENEFITS

Despite the challenges, there are many obvious benefits to community partnerships, too numerous for this chapter and better addressed by other authors. A few broad categories are presented here, which are related in particular to the entrepreneurial theme.

Entrepreneurial leaders, whether administrators, teachers, or partners, are resource scavengers. When the school budget is limited, community partners are an obvious place to look for new resources. So entrepreneurial leaders are more likely to pursue partners, explore ways to enlarge the partnerships, and find strategic ways to use the available resources.

Resources include more than just money, equipment, or technology. Some partnerships provided access. For example, the university partner enlisted Dunbar students as early as ninth grade and offered academic support with the promise of automatic entrance to the college for any student who maintained a B-average or better.[45] Other partners helped with networking; the representative from Verizon Corporation, for example, was often able to connect the high school with promising new initiatives across the city. In other words, in terms of Bronfenbrenner's concentric circles, the partners extended the network that surrounded the school and the children.

Many school leaders find they don't have time to maintain these relationships, especially when outside partners expect immediate telephone access or same-day responses to e-mails. In the absence of a full-time boundary-spanner, some principals engage teacher leaders in the partnering work. This worked particularly well throughout the history of Dunbar High School. Teachers appreciated the targeted resources, and partners often found direct access to students' microsystem in this way.

Of course, community partnerships are also a source of knowledge and expertise (without diminishing at all the resident knowledge and expertise of school staff). A math professor from the university came to the high school every week for two years to meet with the math faculty in a community of practice. They respected and trusted his expertise; they also liked the fact that he was independent of central office agendas. As a result, they voluntarily met with him weekly.

Community partnerships offer a safe environment for risk-taking, which is not always easy in public education. To be fair, the central administration of a large school district is not usually designed to be entrepreneurial; instead, efficiency is the goal in regards to compliance and cost-savings. The superintendent's team cannot afford to take major risks when they operate in the public spotlight and are hemmed in by legal stipulations. Given the short tenure of most superintendents, they need sure-fire initiatives with quick results rather than risky, long-term experiments. [46]

Even those who work inside the public schools have to be cautious about taking risks. Teachers worry about performance evaluations and avoid rocking the boat. Principals are isolated, which undermines confidence. However, community partnerships can create a safe environment where experimentation and risk-taking are encouraged and appreciated.

Thirty years at Dunbar High School told the story of how small groups of teachers met with outside partners and experimented with new ways to meet the needs of students in an under-resourced school. School leaders also came to enjoy partnership meetings for all the ways in which they differed from district meetings; they were less supervisory and placed less emphasis on deadlines and benchmarks. They were less threatening. The meetings were an escape, like a breath of fresh air or a liberating place to think entrepreneurially.

Partnerships not only offer a safe place for risk-taking, they are also a rich source for new ideas. Since partners operate outside the school walls, they are less inhibited by state and district education mandates. They can think beyond student achievement test scores. They bring new ideas and new experiences. These scholars located the sources of innovation in their discussion of organizational theory:

> The canonical formal organization with its bureaucratic rigidities is a poor vehicle for learning. Sources of innovation do not reside exclusively inside firms; instead they are commonly found in the interstices between firms, universities, research laboratories, suppliers and customers. [47]

As a result, schools that aspire to be true learning organizations build their Bronfenbrenner networks so they can jump-start innovative thinking. Institutions partner in order tap into "entrepreneurial energy." [48]

The burst of creative thinking which is found at the boundary between organizations has been called the *Medici Effect*. The term comes from the Medici banking family, whose commerce precipitated a collision of cultures in Renaissance Italy and an explosion of world-famous creativity in the arts. [49] Innovation is driven by the intersection of different perspectives. Chapter 5 discussed, for example, how diversity in professional learning communities, whether by content knowledge, grade level, experience, gender, race, or nationality, can lead to fresh thinking. The collision of cultures is an important strategy for breaking associative barriers.

Boundaries are the location of knowledge production. Whether the boundary is ideological, such as the line between what one knows and doesn't yet know, or organizational, between a school and a community partner, this is where new knowledge is generated. The new thinking that occurs along psychological and organizational boundaries is important for learning organizations.

## CONCLUSION

The focus of this chapter has been on school-community partnerships. Most of our examples were small, with the exception of the $1 million gift of the Trefler Foundation, which funded a five-year, three-way partnership between the high school, the university, and the foundation. However, some important partnerships are citywide. In the late 1990s the New England regional accrediting agency had put numerous Boston schools on probation and was putting targeted pressure on the school district. The mayor of Boston hired one of the top superintendents in the country. The district teamed up with the Private Industry Council and secured significant federal and state grant funding for education. Major institutions of higher education and local foundations were coming together to address substantive change in the public school system. As one business participant noted, "The time was ripe—the stars were in alignment—or, if school improvement doesn't happen now, it never will."[50] This was partnering in the extreme at the exosystem level and the results were extraordinary. The Boston Public School system was a finalist for the Broad Foundation prize for district-wide improvement every year starting in 2002, securing the top prize of $1 million in 2006.[51]

Many people cringe at the emphasis on competition in public education (aside from sports, of course), but international competitions on achievement tests, on which American students are perceived to lag, seem here to stay.[52] Competition is normally seen as the antithesis of collaboration, but many leaders are now proclaiming that "collaboration is the new competition."[53] In other words, collaboration (teamwork) is the key to success. The Boston experience in the years from 1996 to 2006, when so many partners came together to help students succeed, is an example of how collaboration is the new competition to make the Boston Public Schools a winner. Once again, as with so much of the literature on leadership, this new angle began in the business world, but the public education system is sure to benefit from an approach that emphasizes partnering, teamwork, and collaboration.

This is happening all across America. *Strive* is one such educational partnership in Cincinnati, Ohio.[54] One really interesting development is the *Striving Together Report Card*, which is an effort to share data transparently among community partners so real progress can be measured and monitored. Rather than hoarding data (and hoping to hide weaknesses), partnering agencies are taking bold steps to share data so they can get on top of intractable problems.

Another example is *Project LIFT*, which is a unique combination of twenty-two public and private organizations focusing both their attention and a budget of $55 million on 7,400 students in the Charlotte-Mecklenburg, North Carolina, school system. In this case, project partners settled on a comprehensive approach that tackles one high school and surrounding feeder schools. One scholar explained the unusual partnership of public and private institutions: "Foundations want to help school districts to take risks they otherwise wouldn't be able to."[55] The partnership provides the boost for entrepreneurial thinking. Charlotte-Mecklenburg, by the way, was another Broad Prize winner in 2011.[56]

Boston College has a long history of investing in school-community partnerships with the Boston Public Schools.[57] In recent years, with support from five local foundations,[58] the college sponsored *City Connects*, which partnered twenty-one schools and 8,900 K–8 students with an assortment of community agencies for surround care service.[59] The program cost about $500 per child.

Comparing outcomes with students from other control schools, researchers found that *City Connects* kids outperformed in math and English, had higher grade point averages, less chronic absenteeism, and were 46 percent less likely to drop out between grades eight and twelve.[60] Well-designed partnerships make a huge difference and are a source for entrepreneurial leadership. Interestingly, *City Connects* employed a director of new practice and a director of implementation, which was confirmation of the emphasis on innovation.

These examples only scratch the surface on what can happen with large-scale city partnerships. The factors which predict and promote this kind of heightened civic capacity, where big educational, corporate, philanthropic, and social service institutions are able to collaborate so effectively, are still largely unknown.[61] Nevertheless, there is growing interest in understanding how to build these "smart education systems," which in some cases include businesses, non-profits, and cultural institutions.[62]

Opportunities do not wait forever. The first chapter pointed out that public schools are not usually considered entrepreneurial. For this reason, many of the big foundations are turning away from traditional public schools and investing in the "competition," which can mean charter schools and private schools as well as non-traditional preparation programs for administrators and teachers.[63] While grant funding for K–12 education quadrupled from 2000 to 2005, the share that went to traditional public education dropped from 40 to 25 percent; these trends have continued in recent years.[64]

If education leaders—whether at the classroom, school, or district level—want to participate in the benefits of community partnerships, they must be bold and quick to respond. Promising partnerships may never get off the ground when entrenched educational bureaucracies are slow to respond, suspicious of alternative ideas, inflexible, territorial, and consumed with competing agendas. No wonder the big funders turn elsewhere. The need for entrepreneurial leadership in public education, as exemplified in this chapter, has never been greater.

## NOTES

1. See, for example, the Comer Schools, the Coalition of Community Schools (http://www.communityschools.org/), or the National Network of Partnership Schools (http://www.csos.jhu.edu/p2000/index.htm).

2. Epstein, J. L., Sanders, M. G., Simon, B., Salinas, K., Jansorn, N., & Van Voorhis, F. (2002). *School, family and community partnerships: Your handbook for action*. Thousand Oaks, CA: Corwin Press.

3. Slater, J. J., & Ravid, R. (2010). *Collaboration in education*. New York: Routledge.

4. Weerts, D. J., & Sandmann, L. R. (2008). Building a two-way street: Challenges and opportunities for community engagement at research universities. *The Review of Higher Education, 32*(1), 73–106.

5. Fidler-Carey, M. (2012). *Partnership work:Conceptualizing the boundary spanner in k–16 educational partnerships*. Ed.D., University of Massachusetts Boston, Boston, MA.

6. Lawson, H. A. (2003). Pursuing and securing collaboration to improve results, p. 45. In M. M. Brabeck, M. E. Walsh & R. E. Latta (Eds.), *Meeting at the hyphen: Schools-universities-communities-professions in collaboration for student achievement and well-being* (Vol. 2, pp. 45–73). Chicago: National Society for the Study of Education.

7. Corrigan, D. (2000). The changing role of schools and higher education institutions with respect to community-based interagency collaboration and interprofessional partnerships. *Peabody Journal of Education, 75*(3), 176–195. doi: http://dx.doi.org/10.1207/S15327930PJE7503_12.

8. Shaker, E. (2006). Who is calling the shots in your school? *Education Canada, 47*(1), 4.

9. What we do. (2011). Retrieved March 11, 2013, from http://www.edufundingpartners.com/what-we-do.

10. Freeman, M. (2012, November 7). Putting brands to work for public schools. *Education Week, 32,* 24.

11. Fullan, M. (2000). The three stories of education reform. *Phi Delta Kappan, 81*(8), 582.

12. Gonsalves, L., & Leonard, J. (2007). *New hope for urban high schools: Cultural reform, moral leadership and community partnership.* Westport, CT: Praeger.

13. Bronfenbrenner, U. (1979). *The ecology of human development: Experiments by nature and design.* Cambridge, MA: Harvard University Press; Weick, K. E. (1982). Management of organizational change among loosely coupled elements. In P. S. Goodman & Associates (Eds.), *Change in Organizations* (pp. 375–408). Washington: Jossey-Bass; Weick, K. E. (1983). Educational organizations as loosely coupled systems. In J. V. Baldridge & T. E. Deal (Eds.), *The dynamics of organizational change in education* (pp. 15–37). Berkeley, CA: McCutchan Publishing Corporation.

14. Epstein, J.

15. Bronfenbrenner, U.

16. Bronfenbrenner also described two larger circles: the *macrosystem,* which encompassed larger societal values and cultural traditions, and the *chronosystem,* which carried the ecological network of relationships backward and forward in time.

17. Gonsalves, L., & Leonard, J.; Leonard, J. (2011). Using Bronfenbrenner's ecological theory to understand community partnerships: An historical case study of one urban high school. *Urban Education, 46*(5), 987–1010. doi: 10.1177/0042085911400337.

18. Weick, K. E. (1982), 381.

19. Weick, K. E. (1982), 380.

20. Gonsalves, L., & Leonard, J.

21. Bronfenbrenner, U., Hypothesis 35.

22. About ISA. Retrieved March 11, 2013, from http://www.studentachievement.org/AboutISA.aspx; About REL-NEI. Retrieved March 11, 2013, from http://www.relnei.org/about-the-rel-program.html.

23. Leonard, J. (2002). History of a high school community, 1950–2000 (Massachusetts). *DAI, 63*(02A), 318.

24. Fullan, M. G. (1993). Why teachers must become change agents. *Educational Leadership, 50*(6), 12–17; Slater, J. J. (2001). The process of change in school-university collaboration. In R. Ravid & M. G. Handler (Eds.), *The many faces of school-university collaboration: Characteristics of successful partnerships* (pp. 11–22). Englewood, CO: Teacher Ideas Press.

25. Fullan, M. (2000).

26. Gonsalves, L., & Leonard, J.; Leonard, J. (2011).

27. Bronfenbrenner, U., 214, Hypothesis 34.

28. About ISA.

29. Leonard, J. (2011).

30. Classroom at the workplace: College prep. Retrieved March 12, 2013, from http://www.bostonpic.org/employers/classroom-workplace-college-prep.

31. Gonsalves, L., & Leonard, J.

32. Teach Next Year. Retrieved March 12, 2013, from http://www.umb.edu/academics/cehd/curriculum/accelerated_programs/teach_next_year.

33. The replication was called the Boston Teacher Residency program: Boston Teacher Residency. Retrieved March 11, 2013, from http://www.bostonteacherresidency.org/.

34. Diana Christian, the enterprising science teacher featured in chapter 5, was a *Teach Next Year* graduate.

35. Freire, P. (1993). *Pedagogy of the oppressed* (M. B. Ramos, Trans. New revised 20th anniversary ed.). New York: Continuum Publishing Company.

36. Readers will recall the discussion in chapter 5, which revealed that collective intelligence increased when members were good at reading one another's emotions (Johnson, 2010).

37. Benson, L., & Harkavy, I. (2003). The role of the American research university in advancing system-wide education reform, democratic schooling, and democracy. In M. M. Brabeck, M. E. Walsh & R. E. Latta (Eds.), *Meeting at the hyphen: Schools-universities-communities-professions in collaboration for student achievement and well-being* (Vol. 2, pp. 94–116). Chicago: National Society for the Study of Education.

38. Benson, L., & Harkavy, I.; Weerts, D. J., & Sandmann, L. R.

39. Benson, L., & Harkavy, I.; Weerts, D. J., & Sandmann, L. R.

40. McCroskey, J. (2003). Challenges and opportunities for higher education. In M. M. Brabeck, M. E. Walsh & R. E. Latta (Eds.), *Meeting at the hyphen: Schools-universities-communities-professions in collaboration for student achievement and well-being* (Vol. 2, pp. 117–139). Chicago: National Society for the Study of Education; Weerts, D. J., & Sandmann, L. R.

41. Hoy, W., & Miskel, C. (2008). *Educational administration: Theory, research, and practice* (8th ed.). New York: McGraw-Hill.

42. Burch, P., & Spillane, J. (2004). *Leading from the middle: Mid-level district staff and instructional improvement.* Chicago, IL: Cross City Campaign for Urban School Reform.

43. Adams, K. (2005). *The sources of innovation and creativity* (p. 59). Washington, DC: National Center on Education and the Economy.

44. Amabile, T. M. (1997). Motivating creativity in organizations: On doing what you love and loving what you do. *California Management Review, 40*(1), 39–58; Amabile, T. M. (1998). How to kill creativity. *Harvard Business Review, 76*(5), 76–87; Johansson, F. (2006). *Medici effect: What elephants and epidemics can teach us about innovation.* Cambridge, MA: Harvard Business Review Press.

45. Admission Guaranteed Program. Retrieved March 12, 2013, from http://www.umb.edu/academics/vpass/support_programs/admissions_guaranteed_program.

46. Hess, F. M. (1999). *Spinning wheels: The politics of urban school reform.* Washington, DC: Brookings Institution Press.

47. Barringer, B. R., & Harrison, J. S. (2000). Walking a tightrope: Creating value through interorganizational relationships. *Journal of Management, 26*(3), 378, quoting Powell, Koput, & Smith-Doerr, 1996, p. 118.

48. Barringer, B. R., & Harrison, J. S., 373.

49. Johansson, F. (2006). *Medici effect: What elephants and epidemics can teach us about innovation.* Cambridge, MA: Harvard Business Review Press.

50. Minihan, C. E. (1999). The Boston Compact: Past, present and future. *Lowell Lecture Series.* Boston: The Boston Society.

51. Boston Public Schools. (2006). *Broad Prize.* Retrieved January 18, 2013, from http://www.bostonpublicschools.org/broad-prize; Map of previous winners. (2013). Retrieved March 11, 2013, from http://www.broadprize.org/past_winners/map.html.

52. The Trends in International Mathematics and Science Study (TIMSS) and the Program for International Student Assessment (PISA ) are the main examples.

53. Hecht, B. (2013, January 10). Collaboration is the new competition. Retrieved from http://blogs.hbr.org/cs/2013/01/collaboration_is_the_new_compe.html.

54. Strive Partnership. Retrieved March 12, 2013, from http://www.strivetogether.org/.

55. Zubrzycki, J. (2013, January 9). School project blurs line between public, private. *Education Week, 22,* 12.

56. Map of previous winners.

57. Brabeck, M. M., Walsh, M. E., & Latta, R. E. (Eds.). (2003). *Meeting at the hyphen: Schools-universities-communities-professions in collaboration for student achievement and well-being* (Vol. 2). Chicago: National Society for the Study of Education; Walsh, M. E., Brabeck, M. M., Howard, K. A., Sherman, F. T., Montes, C., & Garvin, T. J. (2000). The Boston College-Allston/Brighton partnership: Description and challenges. *Peabody Journal of Education, 75*(3), 6–32.

58. New Balance Foundation, Barr Foundation, Strategic Grant Partners, Charles Hayden Foundation, and Ludcke Foundation.

59. *The impact of City Connects: Progress report 2012.* (p. 44). Newton, MA: Boston College Center for Optimized Support.

60. *The impact of City Connects: Progress report 2012.*

61. Stone, C. N. (2001). Civic capacity and urban education. *Urban Affairs Review, 36*(5), 595–619.

62. Rothman, R. (Ed.). (2007). *City schools: How districts and communities can create smart education systems.* Cambridge, MA: Harvard Education Press.

63. Reckhow, S. (2012, October 15). Introducing the boardroom progressives. Retrieved from http://blogs.edweek.org/edweek/rick_hess_straight_up/2012/10/introducing_the_boardroom_progressives.html.

64. Reckhow, S.

# 7

# ENTREPRENEURIAL LEADERSHIP FOR EVERYONE

This book has attempted to dispel misconceptions about entrepreneurial leadership in education, while whetting the appetite for innovative thinking. At the end of an entire book, the notion of entrepreneurial leadership remains both elusive in definition while tantalizingly attractive. The definitions of entrepreneurship still seem to be all over the park. For example, these scholars offered,

> Entrepreneurship has been defined from various perspectives: pursuit of self-interest (Smith, 1776), innovative combinations of available resources (Schumpeter, 1934), uncertainty and risk-bearing activities (Kets de Vries, 1977), risk-avoiding or -minimizing behavior (Smith and Miner, 1985; Leibenstein, 1968), and proactive or opportunity-seeking behavior (Miller, 1983; Stevenson, 1983).[1]

Similarly, another team offered this list of alternative definitions of entrepreneurism:

- Transforming ideas into enterprises that generate economic, intellectual, and social value (Green, 2005)
- Pursuing and carrying out innovations (Shumpeter)
- Perceiving an opportunity and creating an organization to pursue it (Bygrave, 2004)
- Pursuing an opportunity without regard to resources currently controlled (Stevenson & Jarillo, 1990)
- Specializing in taking judgmental decisions about the coordination of scarce resources (Casson, 1982)

- Being able to evaluate and minimize risk within an organization (Palmer, 1971)[2]

These definitions reflect the emphasis that authors place upon the relative importance of innovation, opportunism, risk-taking, and resource management.

Some have attempted to boil entrepreneurialism down to a concise list of behaviors. For example, Knight reviewed the more traditional breakdown of entrepreneurialism into *innovation* and *proactivity*, where the former emphasizes the pursuit of fresh ideas while the latter measures the energy expended for implementation and, sometimes, aggressiveness in beating out other firms.[3] Gupta and his team pictured entrepreneurial leadership as two processes: *scenario enactment*, which involves creating a compelling vision of possibility, and *cast enactment*, which is the recruitment of a team.[4] These Canadian researchers offered a much more detailed list of behaviors for entrepreneurialism in education:

> The first element, *innovative behavior*, is presented as having four attributes: (a) the generation of knowledge and skills within the organization, (b) the imagining of possible futures or "possibilizing," (c) the demonstration of social and political acumen whereby the leader has the ability to communicate effectively and to facilitate constructive relationships with the members of the organization and external communities, and (d) the technical skills needed to act as a change agent. The second element, *networking*, is characterized by two attributes, that is, information acquisition necessary to lead positive change, and successful adaptation to changing conditions through the manifestation of flexible and resilient behaviors. The third element, *time–space communication framework*, employs new technologies to communicate synchronously and asynchronously with local and distributed audiences in ways that reflect temporal variability, for example, intensive and paced time frames for communication. The fourth element, *local–global perspective*, requires entrepreneurs to develop cultural literacies and multidimensional perspectives that enable them to work responsibly with local, national, and global communities. Fifth, the conceptualization of *educational organizations as knowledge centers* encourages all members of organizations to create and mobilize knowledge in the best interests of learning communities. The sixth element, *integrated face-to-face and Internet-based learning*, recognizes the opportunities that the information age presents for educational organizations to succeed in a competitive international environment through the formation of strategic alliances.[5]

These alternative definitions are offered here for a reason. The definitions are important, for they clarify the concept and answer the suspicions of those who doubt the reality of entrepreneurial leadership. They distinguish this style of leadership from other contenders. Definitions invite assessment, for they provide descriptors, which can be measured and quantified.

There are problems, however, with a clean definition for entrepreneurial leadership. As noted earlier, this is an *ex post* concept; one must be successful with at least one innovation to earn the title. No one calls the perennially unsuccessful risk-taker an entrepreneurial leader.

Secondly, entrepreneurs themselves rebel against the neat definitions. Given their rebellious, James Dean nature, they recoil at being categorized. They distinguish themselves by going outside the lines. No sooner is a list created—especially a long list, such as the one noted previously—than they can find exceptions. For this reason, the entrepreneurial personality defies definition.

For that reason, chapter 2 presented a series of gradients along which the entrepreneurial leader might be placed. This allows for movement and variation. No doubt, there are other gradients. Chapter 1 offered a simplistic definition, which tried to avoid the exceptions: "The entrepreneurial leader begins with a question—*how can we do this better?*—and then turns the innovative ideas into policies, programs, and enterprises, which have intellectual, social, and/or economic value."

## MEASUREMENTS

Despite all these doubts, scholars have attempted to measure this thing. One avenue of research has focused on creativity. For example, psychologist E. Paul Torrance developed the Torrance Test of Creativity which could be administered to children or adults. Torrance and others discovered that people use two kinds of thinking when approaching a difficult problem.[6] Convergent thinking refers to problem-solving thought processes that are linear, analytic, and logical. This kind of thinking is often measured with IQ tests. Divergent thinking, however, is more intuitive and allows for multiple solution paths and answers. Divergent thinkers are more likely to break associative barriers and arrive at novel solutions.[7]

Torrance's measurements on four hundred elementary school children in Minneapolis were later linked to adult accomplishments. The correlation between the lifetime creative accomplishments and childhood was more than three times greater than the correlation of tests of creativity to IQ.[8] While Torrance's work was not specifically targeted at entrepreneurial innovativeness, the fact that business people have latched on to his work reveals the close association they place between creativity and innovativeness.

This simple discussion of creativity sheds light on the definitional problems with entrepreneurial leadership. Usually, definitions are the outcome of convergent thinking. The logical mind demands a boiling down of characteristics into a concise definition. However, entrepreneurs are distinguished by divergent thinking, which allows for multiple answers. What kind of definition does this produce—and how does one measure it?

Despite these challenges, there are more measures for entrepreneurialism, which come from the business world. And no wonder, given the monetary possibilities that are afforded by entrepreneurial success. For example, the Entrescale, first postulated in 1977 and since revised, measures the entrepreneurial orientation of a company. The scale is built on the two-part definition of entrepreneurialism offered earlier—*innovativeness* and *proactivity*—and uses only eight questions on a rating scale. For example, subjects read "When confronted with decision-making situations involving uncertainty, my firm . . ." and must position their firm on a rating scale, between two choices, which measure proactivity:

- Typically adopts a cautious, "wait-and-see" posture in order to minimize the probability of making costly decisions, or
- Typically adopts a bold, aggressive posture in order to maximize the probability of exploiting potential opportunities.[9]

Other questions measure innovativeness, such as this one, "In general, top managers in my firm favor":

- A strong emphasis on the marketing of tried and true products and services, or
- A strong emphasis on research and development, technological leadership and innovations.[10]

As a result, one is able to measure the entrepreneurialism of the firm on both innovativeness and proactivity. Knight was interested in the cross-cultural use of the measure with English- and French-speaking populations and found acceptable levels of reliability and validity, which bolstered the use of the scale internationally.

Tests such as these demonstrate that entrepreneurial orientations can be measured in children as well as adults, that the measurements stand up to time, and that they have cross-cultural applicability. The cross-cultural piece bears some explanation.

In the late 1990s scholars surveyed over fifteen thousand mid-level business managers from nine hundred firms in sixty-two different societies around the world in a broad survey of effective leadership.[11] In a subsequent study, other researchers took the 112 leadership behaviors identified and pulled out 19, which they linked to entrepreneurial leadership. Similar to Knight, they found universal endorsement of entrepreneurial leadership as an effective leadership style. However, they also found slight cultural variations. For example, English, German, and Nordic cultures, which shared a Protestant cultural ethic, viewed entrepreneurial leadership more favorably, while "cultures characterized by high power distance, such as the Middle Eastern and Confucian societies, [were] less likely to endorse entrepreneurial leadership."[12]

Evidently, certain cultures are more receptive to entrepreneurial leadership. Similarly, one might surmise that there is a tension between the historic, democratic, egalitarian culture of public education and the American embrace of a Darwinian survival-of-the-fittest world of entrepreneurship.

One of the great fears of entrepreneurial leadership is that it is antidemocratic. Entrepreneurial leaders work in small teams; they are selective about the inner circle, since it is vital to maintain positive energy and forward momentum. There is an old proverb: "If you want to go fast, go alone; if you want to go far, go together." Entrepreneurs often want to jump on opportunities, so speed is essential, which can often mean making solo decisions. Pulling in stakeholders later is important when one wants to build sustainability, but the early stages can be exclusionary.

In reality, entrepreneurial startups may end up with a more democratic culture than older, well-established enterprises. Over thirty years ago, Kanter wrote, "High-innovation companies . . . tend to go further toward an egalitarian, meritocratic ideal than their counterparts."[13] In contrast, many educators complain about rigid, top-down, command-and-control hierarchies common to public schooling. To understand this further, an overview of some global trends is necessary. This chapter will show how new businesses are empowering workers with flexible hours and freedom to work on personal projects.

## ENTREPRENEURIAL DISRUPTIONS

Joseph Schumpeter introduced the concept of creative destruction to the world when he described entrepreneurship in 1942. Sixty years later, Clayton Christensen further developed this idea when he introduced the concept of disruptive innovations.[14] Schumpeter took a big-picture view when he described how a new innovation could open up new markets, thereby upsetting the equilibrium in the established market, setting off a wave of opportunism that eventually leads to a new equilibrium with a new set of winners and losers. Christensen described this process in more detail, which is best explained with an illustration.

A famous example of a disruptive innovation is the cell phone. In the beginning, cell phones were an inferior product; they were large, clunky, expensive, and reception was unreliable. Big, well-established telephone companies saw little threat, and, besides, they were too busy servicing their large customer base, which was perfectly happy with traditional desktop sets. However, cell phones did offer new choices, and they appealed to a niche market of buyers who were away from home or the office or just intrigued with new gadgets. Sales drove improvements to the technology; the phones shrank in size, the batteries lasted longer, and coverage improved. New buyers appeared, including teenagers, who were ignored by the big companies. Choice, rather than reliability, became the driving value. Eventually, cell phones displaced desktop models, leaving the business giants scrambling to play catch-up.

Disruptive innovations represent the little guy, operating "under the radar," who champions a new product which appeals to an unrecognized and previously ignored market. The product eventually grows in popularity and success to challenge the big guys. There is so much in this process that appeals to the democratic tradition that anyone can become a success in America. Small-time entrepreneurs score big. Customers are empowered.

The cell phone, by its very unconnected nature, also opened up new markets for "the little guy" in an amazing demonstration of democratic empowerment. In India, for example, many rural families with products to sell were for decades the victims of the prevailing market. Each season, they carried their products—everything from rice to woven textiles to handmade crafts—into the city and sold at that day's price. However, with the advent of a cheap cell phone, which they often shared with their entire village, they could stay home and track the city prices, waiting for the most opportune moment to bring their products to market. The cell phone empowered thousands of rural Indians.

The personal computer was another disruptive innovation. While IBM, Wang, and Digital dominated the market for mainframe computers, Apple offered a personal computer. The new computer was inferior, since it lacked computing power and didn't come with a service guy who would come out to make repairs. IBM, Digital, and Wang customers were not interested, so they ignored it. However, the Apple computer was cheap and readily portable, so lots of new people found they could buy their own computer. A new market rapidly opened up. Sales drove development, and in no time the desktop computers began to offer computing power that rivaled the mainframes. In time, faithful IBM and Digital customers began to make the switch. The Apple computer was a disruptive innovation that left some big companies unprepared and vulnerable.

Like the cell phone, Apple was able to bring computing power to millions of consumers. As a result, individual customers were able to use their personal computers to run businesses, analyze data, access the Internet, and compete with the big boys. Thousands of "the little guys" were empowered.

There are two forces today which are giving voice to millions and allowing them to participate in the game of life. The first is the entrepreneurial process. Disruptive innovations only work because there is a hidden customer base that has been waiting to be empowered. Whether the disruptive innovation is a cell phone, a food product, a line of clothing, or a musical genre, new customers are finding that their voice and their pocketbook matter.

The second force, of course, is the technological revolution, which has opened the doors of opportunity to millions of people who now have access to information and markets. Through the Internet, everyone can gain the knowledge, training, information, data, and access to markets they need to succeed. Both forces—entrepreneurial innovations and the worldwide web—have uncovered the almost universal desire of people to have a voice in achieving their dreams. Their energy is having revolutionary effects in society, politics, and business.

## SOCIAL EFFECTS

One of the social benefits of this new empowerment is "smart cities." Technological advances alone have enabled city planners to connect cars, buildings, roads, and even street lights so they communicate with each other for better performance. While efficient, this approach still relies heavily on central planning, leaving residents without a voice and ignoring the innovative solutions they might offer. The truly smart cities are connecting their own citizens to give them a voice in daily affairs.[15] In this case,

> People become the agents of change. With proper technical-support structures, the populace can tackle problems such as energy use, traffic congestion, health care and education more effectively than centralized dictates. And residents of wired cities can use their distributed intelligence to fashion new community activities, as well as a new kind of citizen activism.[16]

In Boston, Massachusetts, for example, residents can snap a picture of a pothole or overflowing trash can on their cell phone and relay it directly to city hall to be addressed. In this way, the government has an army of volunteer data collectors who keep central staffers up to date and direct city maintenance efforts. The Massachusetts Bay Transportation Authority (MBTA), which runs hundreds of miles of subways, trolleys, and buses, posted their routes and schedules online, which enabled enterprising tech volunteers to create cell phone apps that would predict the arrival of the next conveyance. Now, there are dozens of available apps, many free to city riders. No one has to miss a bus anymore or wonder when the next train is coming while waiting in the cold. Ingenuity and technology are empowering the average citizen.

When citizens are invited to participate, the result is greater innovation and increased efficiency in addition to a sense of social cohesion and pride that comes from owning part of the process.

## POLITICAL GAINS

In the political sphere, people show the same desire to participate and shape their own destiny. At times, their grassroots activism is wild and unruly, like the Arab Spring that emerged through "a rich ecosystem of Facebook conversations, Twitter outbursts and chat-room plans."[17] At other times, citizen democracy is slower and more subtle.

For over forty years, personal choice has been knocking on the doors of public education. In America, families can choose to enroll their children in public, private, or parochial schools—or they can home school their children. Many city residents choose to move to the suburbs to raise their children in a safer environment where they can send them to better schools. Suburban schools usually offer more choices in curriculum as well.

Boston has struggled to balance parental choice with central control for years. In the 1980s Boston created magnet schools, which were smaller and offered a thematic approach to education, to keep families in the city. The Academy of Public Service was an example. At the close of the 1980s, Boston introduced a controlled choice plan, which allowed parents to choose the school they wanted for their child instead of being assigned to a neighborhood school, which sometimes lacked quality.[18] For minority parents, especially, this was a huge opportunity. In the same time period, the district introduced school-based management and shared decision-making, which sought to empower parents. Other cities followed similar patterns of empowerment.

In this season of empowerment, the first charter schools in America were started in the early 1990s. Boston was no exception, but the city responded in a very creative way: the district and the teachers union signed a contract that provided for the creation of a handful of "pilot" schools, which were charter-like but still under district supervision.[19] No one knew if charter schools would prove to be a truly disruptive innovation, but Boston did not wait to find out. Many interpreted this as a very savvy, proactive decision on their part. The pilot school idea was studied and duplicated all over the country.

From an economic and social perspective, charter schools have proven to be a disruptive innovation. They appeal to an audience that is traditionally underserved: namely inner city families. They are also a threat to the traditional system of public education since they drain away students and dollars from districts that are often shrinking. Charter school enrollments have increased steadily in Boston.

For Boston, as with IBM, Digital, and Wang, there is a danger when the big players do not pay careful attention to innovations that appear on the horizon. The expert on disruptive innovations warned,

> One word of warning: in our studies of this challenge, we have never seen a company succeed in addressing a change that disrupts its mainstream values without the personal, attentive oversight of the CEO—precisely because of the power of values in shaping the normal resource allocation process. Only the CEO can ensure that the new organization gets the required resources and is free to create processes and values that are appropriate to the new challenge. CEOs who view spinouts as a tool to get disruptive threats off their personal agendas are almost certain to meet with failure. We have seen no exceptions to this rule.[20]

The Boston pilots, which admittedly were a "spinout," are now nearly twenty years old. Nevertheless, charter schools have continued to grow in Boston and, contrary to data from other parts of the country, they are succeeding. One recent study, relying on random student assignments, found Boston charter school students outperforming students in pilot schools and traditional schools. For example, middle school Black students who spent one year in a charter school were able to cut the Black-White achievement gap in half.[21] This is astounding progress.

Boston has responded creatively and aggressively with decentralization, small school restructuring, theme-based academies, and new student assignment plans. There is no question that the advent of charter schools was one factor that has driven innovation in Boston.

This is not written to champion charter schools, which defy simplistic summarizations. Worthy evaluations from across the country offer a mixed record on charter school accomplishments. Advocates of traditional schools often point to a democratic tradition, dating back to the 1800s, of providing a common school education, free of charge, for all American children. Charter schools are portrayed as a threat to this democratic tradition. What is less mentioned is that the original Horace Mann schools were largely independent and locally controlled, just like charter schools; the superstructure of superintendents and central office bureaucracies was only added later.

Today, many parents are voting for charter schools—both in public elections and by enrolling their children. What could be more democratic? Charter schools represent a disruptive innovation, fueled by public demand, which will continue to threaten unless the traditional public school system learns to act entrepreneurially. And this is being followed by other, equally important threats, such as home schooling and online courses, which can be purchased across the country. These innovations are empowering the customer base of students and families.

For many years, America was first in the world for entrepreneurship. This was the place to come if one wanted to succeed. America has taken great pride in her tradition. Now, however, entrepreneurial thinking is under threat in the one place where it ought to be most prevalent. While innovations—disruptive innovations—are breaking out all around, disruptive innovations, educators in traditional systems are debating how much innovation they can handle. Increasingly, the public perception is that entrepreneurship is impossible in public education.

This must change. Entrepreneurship in public education not only offers the possibility of making schools more participative but also addresses a universal need of the stakeholders—the families, students, teachers, administrators, and community partners—to be part of the solution.

## ECONOMICS

One of the most interesting phenomena in recent years is an almost universal drive to participate entrepreneurially in the global economy. People long to have control of their lives and to determine their own future. The United States has always been known as a well-spring of entrepreneurship. However, there is another, even stronger surge of entrepreneurship, which is taking place all over the world.

The world is full of people who work "under-the-table," providing products or services for cash and not reporting the income to the government. Examples include the child's lemonade stand down the street, the boy who shovels a driveway for twenty dollars, or maybe a plumbing friend who fixes a leak on the weekend for a cash payment. For many people around the world, however, this is their only income. They earn their living in a hidden economy that is unregistered, unregulated, and almost entirely beyond taxation. Their numbers are not small. In 2009 the Organization of Economic Cooperation and Development (OECD) estimated that 1.8 billion people, or half the workers of the world, are involved in this kind of economy. [22]

This informal economy has been called "l'économie de la débrouillardise," or System D, from the French word—le débrouillard—for a person who is especially resourceful and motivated. [23] The former French colonies took this word to describe "the ingenuity economy, the economy of improvisation and self-reliance, the do-it-yourself, or DIY, economy." [24]

This shadow economy is only beginning to attract attention. The economy exists everywhere in the world, including North America and Europe, but it is especially dominant in Africa and Asia, especially in "squatter communities or shanty-towns" where one-seventh of the world lives. [25] In Lagos, Nigeria, for example, "70 to 80 percent of the working people in the city are part of the informal economy." [26] The OECD estimates that two-thirds of the world's working force will be found in System D by 2020. [27]

The total value of System D to the international economy is enormous, estimated to be close to $10 trillion, making it the second largest economy in the world, trailing only the United States. [28] Furthermore, the opportunities that are afforded by System D are an important economic safeguard. One German bank, for example, discovered that those European countries where System D was most prevalent were more resilient through the 2008 economic recession. [29]

In the past, this was the economy of desperation, but increasingly, this is the economy of aspiration. [30] System D provides jobs, an income, and a way out of poverty in places where the government and the traditional private sector have not. This is especially true for women. Whether selling scraps rummaged from the city trash heaps or fish caught in the local river, these *débrouillards* carefully budget and expand their enterprises over time to include other employees, cell phones, bank accounts, and credit cards, eventually entering the visible and regulated world of business. [31]

System D embodies the desire for self-determination that is found in human beings. The entrepreneurial energy of System D is an expression of a universal creative drive. In this way, System D is a democratic expression of "power to the people," encouraging men and women all over the world to participate in the global economy. When Mohammed Yunus founded Grameen Bank and invented micro-loans for indigent Bangladeshi women, he tapped into this same drive. [32]

This creative energy is not unlike that found in teacher leaders who long for a greater voice in their schools. This energy is reflected in the principal who wants to take a more enterprising role in school leadership. When students throw themselves into an authentic project, which reflects their concerns and connects to their world, they are expressing the same drive for ownership and expression.

The drive for entrepreneurism in education is not contrary to democracy. Entrepreneurial leadership opens doors and provides options to everyone in public education. Teachers find new ways to serve and grow. Parents and students find new educational opportunities.

System D is the world's largest disruptive innovation. Nothing gives better expression to mankind's need for self-determination. Too often, the public school system has resisted disruptive innovations and insisted instead on conformity and compliance in the name of the common good. The result is a loss of opportunities for stakeholders. One needs a more generous view of things. Alfonso Morales (professor of urban planning at University of Wisconsin–Madison) said, "We need to go from a purely enforcement mentality to a mentality of 'Let's try to enlarge the pie and increase people's share of it.'" [33]

## THE CREATIVE WORLD

This chapter makes the case that entrepreneurial thinking gives voice to some fundamentally important human desires. One is the desire for self-determination. Another important human drive, which is related, is the need to create and to express oneself. Humans have the wonderful ability to take an idea—a story line, a vision, a melody—and turn it into a beautiful work of art. Entrepreneurial leaders are imaginative, creative people who are driven by an idea and not hampered by the lack of resources. They are visionary because they see over the boundaries and beyond the horizon. They can sense the final product and assemble an innovation where nothing existed before. Like artists, they are inspired.

Previous chapters have alluded to creative thinking processes, which are common among entrepreneurial leaders. Chapter 3 noted that creative people are not afraid of disagreeing or challenging an idea.[34] They enjoy looking for alternative solutions. This is a kind of divergent thinking, which was described earlier in this chapter.[35] Chapter 5 presented brainstorming as a creative strategy.[36]

Creative people challenge boundaries. They do not limit their thinking to the boundaries of conventional thought. They are more likely to think outside the box—where the box describes the set of mental associations that are normally clustered around a concept, a set which leads to predictable answers. Creative people practice divergent thinking; they split from the pack mentality and look in new directions. They break down associative barriers, which opens the way for new ideas.[37]

In the process of crossing boundaries, creative people find new ideas and new materials. Their divergent thinking allows them to juxtapose elements or ideas that are not normally associated. One recalls mixed media works of art, where various materials, such as seashells, string, fur, wire, or electronics, are mingled on one canvas to create something unique and provocative. But the juxtaposition is more than that. For example, Canadian artist Steven Rhude painted a colorful Nova Scotian coastal fishing cabin in front of New York City's staid, grey Guggenheim Museum to jar the viewer's imagination. The contrast of color and culture raises so many questions. Would the inhabitants ever really visit one another? Would the expertise of the one ever be welcome in the other? The painting raises questions about cultures, which are too often mutually exclusive.

Entrepreneurial experts seek to understand the creative process. In a study of five thousand top executives, entrepreneurial guru Clayton Christensen and his team sought to identify the particular skills of innovative leaders.[38] They narrowed the list to five items, which they presented in a book called *The Innovator's DNA*.

- *Questioning*, which allows innovators to challenge the status quo and consider new possibilities.
- *Observing*, which helps innovators detect small behavioral details—in the activities of customers, suppliers, and other companies—that suggest new ways of doing things.
- *Networking*, which permits innovators to gain radically different perspectives from individuals with diverse backgrounds.

- *Experimenting*, which prompts innovators to relentlessly try out new experiences, take things apart, and test new ideas.
- *Associational Thinking*—drawing connections between questions, problems, or ideas from unrelated fields—is triggered by questioning, observing, networking, and experimenting and is the catalyst for creativity. [39]

The last item in this list is the outcome of the previous four habits. Associational thinking, in other words, is "triggered" by questioning, observing, networking, and experimenting. Many of these behaviors were first described in chapter 1. Entrepreneurs are always questioning: "how can we do this better?" They are always on the lookout for a better idea. They network feverishly to gain perspective and more resources. Experimentation is central to the innovative process. Christensen and his team believed these skills could be learned.

School leaders who hope to run entrepreneurial organizations that break with tradition should teach and model associational thinking at every level of the enterprise. These skills are crucial to the learning organization. For example, questioning is indispensable for classroom learning. Effective teachers carefully design questions that challenge assumptions and unearth misconceptions. Students need to ask questions to learn, which requires a safe culture where differences of opinion, risk-taking, and mistakes are allowed.

Observing is fundamental to differentiated instruction, whether the teacher is taking note of individual learning styles or different outcomes on formative assessments. Networking was a prominent theme in both chapter 5, which argued for the value of diverse teaching teams, and in chapter 6 on partnerships. Experimentation is standard fare in the science classrooms, but every teacher researcher does the same thing regardless of content area. All these skills are not foreign to public education; they are just not practiced with determination.

In organizations where innovation is valued, leaders recognize that entrepreneurial thinking comes in many shapes and sizes. This is sort of like the "multiple intelligences" of entrepreneurialism. For example, Tom Kelley and Jonathan Littman, authors of *The Ten Faces of Innovation*, focused on the personalities required for entrepreneurial success. Taking a big-picture portrayal of the entire entrepreneurial process, they described the ten "personas" of the entrepreneurial enterprise. There were learners who did the creative work; this group included the anthropologist, the experimenter, and the cross-pollinator. In turn, the organizers built an enabling company culture; they included hurdlers, collaborators, and directors. Finally, the builders focused on implementation; these were the architects, set designers, storytellers, and caregivers.[40]

The terms for these ten types of innovators are creative, and they make the point that entrepreneurialism is not one person with a good idea. A team approach is required. The school organization that aspires to be more entrepreneurial will look to recognize and develop these personality types in the students and teachers.

Entrepreneurial organizations regularly look for strategies to increase innovative thinking. For example, the authors of *The Innovator's DNA* offered some tips for associational thinking.[41] Tip number one was to "force new associations" by "combining things that we would never naturally combine."[42] They gave a silly example:

> To practice forced associations, first consider a problem or challenge you or your company is facing. Then try the following exercises to force an association that you normally wouldn't make: Pick up a product catalog and turn to the twenty-seventh page. What does the first product that you see have to do with the problem you are thinking about? Does the way it solves a problem for a customer have anything to do with your problem?[43]

Tip number two was equally fun: take on the persona of a different company. The authors described one company where

> people haul out large boxes full of hats, shirts, and other things from some of the most innovative companies in the world, like Apple and Virgin. They put on the clothing and assume the persona of someone from that company to look at their challenge from an entirely different perspective.[44]

No doubt, some educators will find these tips more amusing than helpful. Nevertheless, they reinforce the fact that unorthodox tactics are sometimes needed to stimulate fresh thinking.

The third tip is to "generate metaphors: to escape from idea ruts, engage in activities that provoke an analogy or metaphor for your company's products or services."[45] One school posted images of tools from a carpenter's box—a hammer, screwdriver, pliers, saw, and file—and asked faculty to gather around the picture that best described their teaching philosophy. The exercise increased mutual respect and understanding, which was important for this community of practice, but also helped teachers look at their own profession in a new light. "What if I were more like a hammer than a screwdriver in the classroom?"

There were other tips. Tip number four was build a "curiosity box," which was a collection of oddities, easily found in yard sales or thrift shops. Imagine a principal's office where the desk or shelf features a bird house, an automobile spring, a yo-yo, and a Florida conch. "Pull out unique items randomly when confronted with a problem or opportunity . . . to provoke a new angle on an old problem."[46] This unorthodox decorating scheme would make perfect sense to artists who often fill their studios with unusual and seemingly irrelevant objects. They are avenues for associational thinking.

And finally tip number five was to SCAMPER, which was an acronym for "substitute; combine; adapt; magnify, minimize, modify; put to other uses; eliminate; reverse, rearrange."[47] Any or all of these techniques can open doors to new ways of thinking about a problem.

If all this sounds like just so much play, well, there is a reason for that. Roy Lichtenstein, the pop artist who combined images of advertising stock with comic book art, referred to his studio as his "playpen."[48] This is not the first word that comes to mind for most principals or school teachers as they approach their place of work, which is unfortunate. Children do think in terms of play—and research increasingly verifies the importance of play in the learning process.[49] Perhaps this explains some of the disengagement seen among students.

The reader might dismiss these tips as silly game play, but artists are less likely to belittle them. There are sound reasons to hold on to that childish sense of play. Chapter 1 introduced Joi Ito, the director of the MIT Media Lab, the innovative powerhouse in Cambridge, Massachusetts. Ito understood the importance of childlike qualities:

> "Neoteny" is the retention of childlike attributes in adulthood. As a child you learn, you have wonder, you're curious, and every day's a new day. But at some point you become an adult. And as an adult you focus on producing, reproducing, protecting. In the old days, the world didn't change very much, so once you became a plumber, you didn't really need to learn that much more about plumbing. Today you have to keep learning, and learning is somewhat of a childlike behavior. We want the Media lab to be more like kindergarten and less like a lumber mill.[50]

The games just mentioned are examples of exercises that anyone can use to help think outside the box. Some companies forgo the games but aim instead for a company culture that encourages the imagination.

The Google company policy that encourages employees to spend 20 percent of their paid time working on their own projects is now well-known and mimicked around the world in entrepreneurial startups.[51] On a similar vein, the 1,300 employees at the Patagonia clothing company enjoy a "Let My People Go Surfing" flex-time policy, which encourages them to go surfing, hiking, or whatever to spark the imagination so they return with greater productivity. Entrepreneurs are highly motivated individuals. One retailer, Zappos, maximizes motivation by offering new employees $3,000 to turn around and leave the company. They follow up a year later with a $4,000 offer for veteran employees to walk away. As a result, only the committed remain.[52] Starwood Hotels and Resorts, which operates hotels around the world, keeps moving their corporate headquarters, first to Shanghai and, more recently, to Dubai, to stir the creative juices. In each setting, they find that different staff members shine and unanticipated ideas emerge.[53]

These are costly but serious efforts to strike the innovative spark that will keep organizations on the cutting edge. This is the equivalent of a public school district offering short-term sabbaticals to innovative educators or providing incentives for tenured but tired employees to leave. What would happen if superintendents gathered mid-level managers who work in the matrix, instead of their executive team to explore innovative solutions? How about moving the district headquarters to a new and more accessible location—all within a culture that constantly asks, "How can we do this better?" and is willing to recognize and reward sound answers. These ideas only make sense when there is a desperation to find new solutions for intractable school problems.

Business scholars who analyzed the resources, processes, and values of corporate organizations on a flexibility spectrum found that resources were most flexible and values were least flexible. In other words, it was comparatively easy to increase, decrease, or redirect the budget to new purposes, somewhat harder to change core institutional processes, and extremely difficult to change the institutional values that underwrite that work.[54]

Any school district can throw more money at a problem, such as the achievement gap, bullying, college readiness, or how to help limited English proficient (LEP) students from dozens of nations master a new language. Changing procedures and processes whereby bullying is addressed or curriculum is aligned for college readiness is more difficult. However, changing the invisible culture of attitudes and beliefs that reinforces race-related achievement gaps or imprisons LEP students in a world of low expectations is hardest of all to change. This is the challenge of adaptive work. This is why serious, dramatic steps that will stimulate fresh thinking are so important.

## CONCLUSION

This chapter considered the ways in which entrepreneurism addresses universal human needs to engage in the democratic processes of participation, choice, and self-determination. In addition, entrepreneurism gives voice to mankind's need for creativity and self-expression. The chapter concluded with a sample of innovative personality types, tips for creativity, and examples of cultures that are deliberately entrepreneurial.

Some of these ideas are more expensive than others. Those who are anxious will be consoled by this final tip for associational thinking:

> I think that they cannot replace the most important method for stimulating associational thinking—READING. Individuals can derive tremendous value from making a habit of reading voraciously about what is going on in other industries and disciplines. We should not trap ourselves by only reading in our own specialized domain.[55]

Fittingly, this book on entrepreneurial leadership for public education ends with a reading tip. Far too often, educators confine their reading. They read student papers, school reports, and district directives but don't lift their eyes to the horizon to see what's coming at the state, national, or international level in education. And they might never think of reading across boundaries into other domains.

This book has visited a lot of alternative worlds, including the domains of business, economics, ecobiology, sociology, psychology, and art. More than anything, this book has been an exercise in associational thinking. Hopefully, some readers have come to recognize their own entrepreneurial stirrings and will be encouraged to lead accordingly.

## NOTES

1. Gupta, V., MacMillan, I. C., & Surie, G. (2004). Entrepreneurial leadership: Developing and measuring a cross-cultural construct. *Journal of Business Venturing, 19*(2), 242.

2. Borasi, R., & Finnegan, K. (2010). Entrepreneurial attitudes and behaviors that can help prepare successful change-agents in education. *The New Educator, 6,* 3.

3. Knight, G. A. (1997). Cross-cultural reliability and validity of a scale to measure firm entrepreneurial orientation. *Journal of Business Venturing, 12,* 213–225.

4. Gupta, V., MacMillan, I. C., & Surie, G., 247.

5. Scott, S., & Webber, C. F. (2013). Entrepreneurialism for Canadian principals: Yesterday, today and tomorrow. *Journal of Research on Leadership Education, 8*(1), 115. doi: 10.1177/1942775112443438.

6. Reinartz, W. (2013, March 13). Measuring creativity: We have the technology. Retrieved from http://blogs.hbr.org/cs/2013/03/measuring_creativity_we_have_t.html.

7. Readers may recall the story told in chapter 2 of the man with the car who was frustrated by his irresponsible family members. Rather than facing this adaptive challenge, the entrepreneurial leader was exploring alternative solutions.

8. Reinartz, W.

9. Knight, G. A., 224.

10. Knight, G. A., 223.

11. Readers will recall from chapter 3 that entrepreneurial thinking, or intrapreneurship, is best exercised at the middle management level in large businesses.

12. Gupta, V., MacMillan, I. C., & Surie, G., 256.

13. Kanter, R. M. (1983). *The change masters: Innovation and entrepreneurship in the American corporation* (p. 32). New York: Simon & Schuster, Inc.

14. Christensen, C. M., & Overdorf, M. (2000). Meeting the challenge of disruptive change. *Harvard Business Review, 78*(2), 66–76.

15. Ratti, C., & Townsend, A. (2011). The social nexus. *Scientific American, 305*(3), 42–48.

16. Ratti, C., & Townsend, A., 44.

17. Ratti, C., & Townsend, A., 42.

18. Leonard, J. (2002). History of a high school community, 1950–2000 (Massachusetts). *DAI, 63*(02A), 318.

19. The strengths and limitations of pilot programs were discussed in chapter 3.

20. Christensen, C. M., & Overdorf, M., 74.

21. Abdulkadiroglu, A., Angrist, J., Cohodes, S., Dynarski, S., Fullerton, J., Kane, T., et al. (2013). *Informing the debate: Comparing Boston's charter, pilot and traditional schools* (p. 56). Boston, MA: The Boston Foundation.

22. Neuwirth, R. (2011b). The shadow superpower. *Foreign Policy*. Retrieved from http://www.foreignpolicy.com/articles/2011/10/28/black_market_global_economy#.Tq_s2CCPKcw.email.

23. Neuwirth, R. (2011b), 17.

24. Neuwirth, R. (2011b), 17–18.

25. Neuwirth, R. (2011a). Global bazaar. *Scientific American, 305*(3), 58.

26. Neuwirth, R. (2011a), 62.

27. Neuwirth, R. (2011b).

28. Neuwirth, R. (2011b).

29. Neuwirth, R. (2011b).

30. Neuwirth, R. (2011b).

31. This is not meant to recommend garbage-picking as a great opportunity. Rather, the fact that enterprising people will resort even to this is evidence of the universal desire to succeed in spite of the system and to control one's destiny.

32. Yunus, M. (2003). *Banker to the poor: Microlending and the battle against world poverty*. New York: Public Affairs.

33. Neuwirth, R. (2011a), 63.

34. Amabile, T. M. (1997). Motivating creativity in organizations: On doing what you love and loving what you do. *California Management Review, 40*(1), 39–58.

35. Reinartz.

36. Adams, K. (2005). *The sources of innovation and creativity* (p. 59). Washington, DC: National Center on Education and the Economy.

37. Johansson, F. (2006). *Medici effect: What elephants and epidemics can teach us about innovation*. Cambridge, MA: Harvard Business Review Press.

38. Christensen, C. M., Gregersen, H. B., & Dyer, J. H. (2011). The innovator's DNA: Mastering the five skills of disruptive innovators. *Harvard Business School Press Books*, 304.

39. Upbin, B. (2011). The five habits of highly innovative leaders. *Forbes*. Retrieved from http://www.forbes.com/sites/bruceupbin/2011/07/20/the-five-habits-of-highly-innovative-leaders/.

40. Kelley, T., & Littman, J. (2005). *The ten faces of innovation: IDEO's strategies for defeating the devil's advocate and driving creativity throughout your organization*. New York: Currency/Doubleday.

41. The tips, unlike the study on associational thinking, have not been experimentally proven.

42. Dyer, J., Gregersen, H., & Christensen, C. M. (2011, July 19). An innovator's guide: 5 ways to think outside the box, para. 6. Retrieved from http://www.cnbc.com/id/43809587/An_Innovator039s_Guide_5_Ways_to_Think_Outside_the_Box.

43. Dyer, J., Gregersen, H., & Christensen, C. M., para. 7.

44. Dyer, J., Gregersen, H., & Christensen, C. M., para. 8.

45. Dyer, J., Gregersen, H., & Christensen, C. M., para. 9.

46. Dyer, J., Gregersen, H., & Christensen, C. M., para. 11.

47. Dyer, J., Gregersen, H., & Christensen, C. M., para. 13.

48. Lichtenstein, D. (2001). The misanthrope manqué: Through a glass lightly (p. 20). In R. Fitzpatrick & D. Lichtenstein (Eds.), *Roy Lichtenstein: Interiors* (p. 104). Manchester, VT: Hudson Hills.

49. Lester, S., & Russell, W. (2010). Children's right to play: An examination of the importance of play in the lives of children worldwide. *Working Papers in Early Childhood Development* (Vol. 57, p. 80). The Hague, NL: Bernard van Leer Foundation.

50. Jannot, M. (2012). Making gadgets great. *Popular Science*, p. 20. Retrieved January 26, 2013, from http://www.popsci.com/bown/2011/innovator/making-gadgets-great.

51. This is really not a new idea; the 3M company was doing this back in the 1950s. Berkun, S. (2008). Thoughts on Google's 20% time. Retrieved from http://scottberkun.com/2008/thoughts-on-googles-20-time.

52. Ransom, D. (2011, April 11). Finding success by putting company culture first. *Entrepreneur*. Retrieved from http://www.entrepreneur.com/article/219509.

53. Paasschen, F. v. (2013, March 13). Why we're relocating our HQ to Dubai for one month. Retrieved from http://blogs.hbr.org/cs/2013/03/why_were_relocating_our_hq_to_dubai.html.

54. Christensen, C. M., & Overdorf, M.

55. Roberto, M. (2012, December 14). *Associational thinking and creativity*. Retrieved from http://michael-roberto.blogspot.com/2012/12/associational-thinking-creativity.html.

# INDEX

# ABOUT THE AUTHOR

**Jack Leonard** has served in education for forty-five years, from preschool to graduate school, as a teacher, an administrator, and a school founder. He now teaches and conducts research on leadership and school partnerships for the Leadership in Urban Schools program at the University of Massachusetts Boston.